Supporting Primary Teaching and Learning

TEACHING ASSISTANTS

Supporting Primary Teaching and Learning

 Fiona Hall, Duncan Hindmarch, Doug Hoy & Lynn Machin

TEACHING ASSISTANTS

First published in 2015 by Critical Publishing Ltd

British Library Cataloguing in Publication Data
A CIP record for this book is available from the British Library

ISBN: 978-1-909682-89-4

This book is also available in the following e-book formats:

MOBI ISBN: 978-1-909682-90-0
EPUB ISBN: 978-1-909682-91-7
Adobe e-reader ISBN: 978-1-909682-92-4

The rights of Fiona Hall, Duncan Hindmarch, Doug Hoy and Lynn Machin to be identified as the Authors of this work have been asserted by them in accordance with the Copyright, Design and Patents Act 1988.

Cover and text design by Greensplash Limited
Project management by Out of House Publishing
Printed and bound in Great Britain by Bell & Bain, Glasgow

Critical Publishing
152 Chester Road
Northwich
CW8 4AL
www.criticalpublishing.com

MIX
Paper from
responsible sources
FSC® C007785
FSC
www.fsc.org

Contents

Meet the authors

Fiona Hall is an award leader for the BA in education at Staffordshire University and teaches on the BA in education and BA in early childhood studies. She has several years' direct experience of working in the primary sector as well as in further education. She has also prepared HLTA candidates for assessment and she is still currently an assessor.

Duncan Hindmarch is award leader for the Foundation Degree in education at Staffordshire University. He has over 15 years' teaching experience, having worked overseas and in the UK. With a background in teaching English for speakers of other languages (TESOL), he has been involved in developing and delivering TESOL and initial teacher education (ITE) programmes since 2005.

Doug Hoy is a tutor on the Foundation Degree in education for Staffordshire University and the PCGE (post-16) in the northwest of England. He is an educator with over 25 years' experience. He has taught at all levels from infants (KS1) to post-graduate study, both in the UK and overseas, and is also currently delivering and assessing the new functional skills curriculum for adults.

Lynn Machin is an award leader for ITE (post-compulsory), senior lecturer and an MA, EdD, PhD supervisor within the School of Education at Staffordshire University. Her previous roles include those of course leader for both Foundation Degree and level 3 teaching assistants awards. Her particular research interest is the exploration of how students can develop their capacities to learn and to develop as self-directed and autonomous learners. She has written and co-authored several books for teachers within FE, including *A Complete Guide to the Level 5 Diploma in Education and Training*.

Acronyms

AfL	Assessment for Learning
AO	awarding organisation
ATL	Association of Teachers and Lecturers
ADHD	Attention Deficit Hyperactivity Disorder
ARG	Assessment Reform Group
ASD	Autistic Spectrum Disorder
AYPH	Association for Young People's Health
BBC	British Broadcasting Corporation
CAF	Common Assessment Framework
CPAG	Child Poverty Action Group
CPPD	continuing personal and professional development
CRB	Criminal Records Bureau
DCSF	Department for Children, Schools and Families
DfE	Department for Education
DfEE	Department for Education and Employment
DfES	Department for Education and Skills
DH	Department for Health
DBS	Disclosure and Barring Service
EAL	English as an Additional Language
ECM	Every Child Matters
EHC(P)	Education, Health and Care (Plan)
EHRC	Equality and Human Rights Commission
ELG	Early Learning Goals
ETF	Education and Training Foundation
EYFS	Early Years Foundation Stage
HLTA	Higher Level Teaching Assistant
ICT	information and communications technology
IEP	Individual Education Plan

ISA	Independent Safeguarding Authority
LADA	Local Authority Designated Officer
LSA	Learning Support Assistant
LSCB	Local Safeguarding Children Boards
NASUWT	National Association of Schoolmasters Union of Women Teachers
NC	national curriculum
NHS	National Health Service
NSPCC	National Society for the Prevention of Cruelty to Children
OECD	Organisation for Economic Co-operation and Development
Ofsted	The Office for Standards in Education, Children's Services and Skills
ONS	Office for National Statistics
PECS	Pictorial Exchange Communication System
PISA	Programme of International Student Assessment
PoS	Programme of Study
QCA	The Qualifications and Curriculum Authority
RDI	Relationship Development Intervention®
SCR	Serious Case Reviews
SEN	special educational needs
SENCO	Special Educational Needs Co-ordinator
SEND	Special Educational Needs and Disabilities
SENDA	Special Educational Needs and Disability Act
SENTA	Special Educational Needs Teaching Assistant
STA	Standards and Testing Agency
TA	Teaching Assistant
TAC	Team Around the Child
TDA	Training and Development Agency for Schools
TES	Times Educational Supplement
UNCRC	United Nations Convention on the Rights of the Child
ZPD	Zone of Proximal Development

Introduction

THE AIM OF THIS BOOK

As a teaching assistant (TA), you are a key professional within the education workforce. Your flexibility and ability to take on a variety of roles and responsibilities enable you to provide targeted support to learners. Your role is therefore vital to your school's provision and success.

Although additional support staff working in school is not a new concept, the greatest increase arose as a result of the changes to teachers' conditions in 2003 in the National Agreement (Department for Education and Skills (DfES), 2003). Additional staff began to be employed in schools to take on a range of tasks to assist teachers, many of which were administrative in nature, allowing teachers time to plan and assess. As time has passed, this role has developed, and support staff or TAs are increasingly involved in direct support of the teacher, assisting the learning of individuals and groups as well as being responsible for a range of specific, targeted interventions. Furthermore, TAs may have a great deal of responsibility for supporting children with special educational needs (SEN), often regardless of their level of qualification or relevant experience.

As a TA, in order to do a good job, it is imperative that you know what is expected of you and that you have close liaison with your classteachers or the teacher responsible for SEN. Additionally, training on the relevant interventions and self-study regarding such things as school practice, behaviour management, the curriculum and SEN may well be needed to complement an in-depth working knowledge of the procedures and policies of the school you are in. A good grounding in English and mathematics is necessary and you may also find that you have a specific skill that your school begins to draw upon, such as being good at sport. You will be a role model to the children, so it is important that you feel comfortable with your role and take on board the need to ensure things like your competency in the English language and your ability to dress appropriately for the surroundings. The Office for Standards in Education (Ofsted), responsible for school inspections, is increasingly interested in the deployment of TAs, so it is good to feel confident and clear about what you do.

This book has been written for people who want to develop their skills and knowledge regarding supporting teaching and learning in primary schools. Specifically, it helps to develop skills beyond level 3 and is therefore particularly beneficial for those beginning study at higher education level. The book is divided into chapters, which cover a number of relevant topics that will assist both your study and your practice. You may be considering a long-term goal of training to become a teacher, with gaining Higher Level Teaching Assistant (HLTA) status as an intermediate objective. With this in mind, the chapters also have links to the HLTA standards. Regardless of your career aspirations, this book aims to support your professional development as a TA as well as help you to enhance your career prospects.

CONTENT AND STRUCTURE

Chapter 1 Reflective practice and study skills

This chapter introduces a range of theories and strategies that can assist your understanding and application of reflection. It also explores how reflective practice can help you to identify any areas for improvement and subsequently to consider what you need to do for your continuing personal and professional development (CPPD). Finally, and in relation to your CPPD, this chapter provides guidance on the development of study skills, for example, time management, referencing and grammar. Activities and examples relating to reflection, CPPD and study skills can be found throughout the chapter.

Chapter 2 Education, learning and development

This looks at the theoretical background behind teaching and learning, and considers how children learn and the barriers that may exist. It provides a critical reflection on a number of educational theories.

Chapter 3 Behaviour management

Chapter 3 is concerned with behaviour management. It outlines some of the reasons behind poor behaviour and helps you gain an understanding of what might trigger it. The chapter considers how the environment can influence behaviour and includes some detailed strategies for dealing with problem behaviour.

Chapter 4 Safeguarding and child protection

Chapter 4 considers the area of safeguarding and child protection. It identifies some of the key cases and subsequent legislation that have influenced the area of safeguarding, as well as outlining your role and responsibilities. It clearly describes what action you should take should you see any of the key indicators of abuse and neglect.

Chapter 5 Inclusion and special educational needs

Chapter 5 examines inclusion and SEN. It outlines some of the key legislative changes that have taken place in 2014 and which will impact on schools, in particular the 2014 SEN Code of Practice. Although not an exhaustive list, it examines some of the special educational needs that you are likely to come across in schools, such as Attention Deficit Hyperactivity Disorder and dyslexia, and suggests strategies to support these learners. In addition, when considering inclusion, it is not always about SEN and the chapter covers suggestions for supporting children with English as an Additional Language (EAL) as well as gifted and talented children.

Chapter 6 The curriculum

This chapter examines the purpose of the curriculum. It examines what is taught in schools, by whom and to what ends, as well as who decides what goes in and, just as important, what is left out. It examines opposing viewpoints to the 'new' national curriculum and gives practical examples for applying literacy and numeracy requirements in your workplace.

Chapter 7 Assessment and accountability

Assessing learning, either formally or informally, is a key part of your professional role. This chapter provides an overview of the principles of assessment to help you reflect on and develop your practice. You will consider the benefits and challenges of assessment of learning and assessment for learning. This chapter also looks at how assessment is central to the curriculum, from early years to Key Stage 2.

Chapter 8 Teamworking

This chapter examines the area of teamworking. In particular, it considers how TAs work in partnership with the classteacher, and the relationships that exist between TAs, learning support assistants (LSAs), learning mentors, teachers and other professionals.

Chapter 9 Career development

This final chapter reviews your rights, roles and responsibilities in the workplace, as well as employment opportunities. As a TA, you are a highly skilled professional and you will have developed a broad range of abilities. This chapter will help you focus on how to develop your role and consider further employment opportunities both within and outside of the education sector.

REFERENCES

Department for Education and Skills (2003) *Raising Standards and Tackling Workload: A National Agreement*. London: Department for Education and Skills. [online] Available at: http://dera.ioe.ac.uk/540/1/081210thenationalagreementen.pdf (accessed October 2014).

1 Reflective practice and study skills

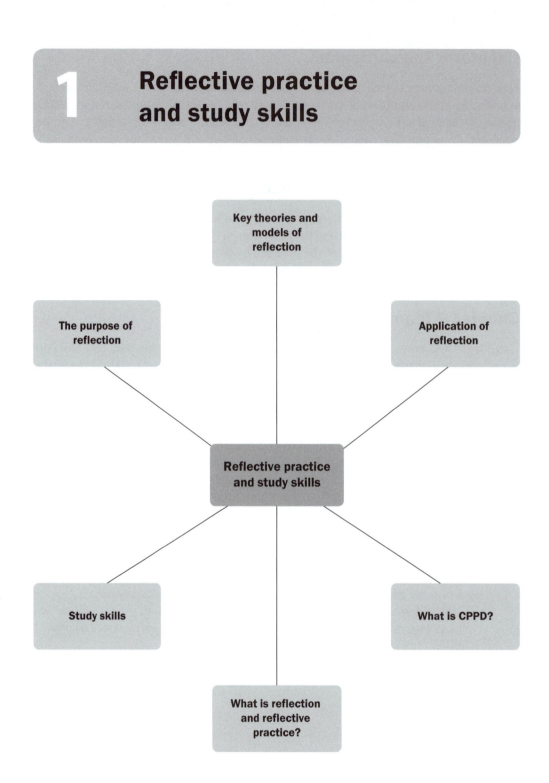

Key theories and models of reflection

The purpose of reflection

Application of reflection

Reflective practice and study skills

Study skills

What is CPPD?

What is reflection and reflective practice?

HLTA STANDARDS

This chapter links to the following HLTA standard (Training and Development Agency for Schools (TDA), 2007, p 97):

7: improve own knowledge and practice including responding to advice and feedback.

The process of reflecting is integral to your professional role and practice, and in this sense underpins all of the HLTA standards.

INTRODUCTION

This chapter introduces a range of theories and strategies that can assist your understanding and application of reflection. It also explores how reflective practice can help you to identify any areas for improvement in order to consider your actions for personal and professional development. It concludes with advice on some vital study skills.

STARTING POINT

○ What do you currently understand by the term *reflection of practice*?

○ In relation to your role as a teaching assistant, what issues do you normally reflect on?

○ What, if any, models of reflective practice are you already aware of?

WHAT IS REFLECTION AND REFLECTIVE PRACTICE?

Reflection and reflective practice are terms that are regularly used by people who have professional roles and responsibilities, which includes you in your role as a teaching assistant (TA). However, what exactly is reflection and reflective practice?

Question

Consider the following statements and decide which one you think best fits the descriptions of *reflection* and *reflective practice*.

Reflection is:

○ looking back wishfully about a situation;

- ○ looking back at a situation from an objective standpoint;

- ○ thinking about an experience and what you did and why you did it.

Reflective practice requires you to:

- ○ think about what it is you are doing;

- ○ do things differently next time;

- ○ challenge your current thinking in order to understand what it is you are doing, why you are doing it and what you need to do differently next time.

Answer

Reflection, in its various guises, is all of the above.

However, although you may look back on a situation and wish you had done something differently, you may not always turn this reflection into action. If you fail to act following your reflections you are likely to have the same experiences again.

Looking back at a situation from an objective standpoint is important because your view of a situation can be obscured by your emotions. However, how do you know that you are being objective? Your current mental models influence your thinking and these models are shaped by your socio-cultural background and experiences, that is, your interactions with various social and cultural events.

Questions

- ○ Consider your own school days. How were you taught? Who was your favourite teacher and what did you like/dislike about school?

- ○ How often do you mentally or verbally make comparisons with the school education that you received and that of children in today's schools? What insights does this give you?

Answers

Your experiences during your school days will have shaped the value and belief systems that you now have as an adult. These will have laid the foundation for some of your assumptions about school and education. Knowing how to reflect can help you to consider and, where necessary, challenge these assumptions so that you can change your thinking and behaviour to improve your practice.

Meta-cognition and reflection

Reflecting about an experience, and thinking about what you did and why you did it, requires the use of your meta-cognitive (thinking about thinking) skills. Using and developing these skills are important parts of the process of reflection and are pivotal to your development as a professional practitioner.

Question

How do you ensure that you review and challenge any stereotypical views that you have?

Answer

You need to dig deep into your thoughts and memory and be honest about any views that you hold. Some of these will be so entrenched in your value system that you may not appreciate that they are based on stereotypical views. An openness to being challenged by others, asking questions, reading literature and engaging in conversations with a diverse range of people can assist you in recognising why you hold your current views. Adapting your mental models when some new thinking occurs leads to *transformative learning* (Mezirow, 1997, p 5), which subsequently helps you to change your behaviour and develop the skills necessary to offer a quality learning experience to the children in your class/es.

KEY THEORIES AND MODELS OF REFLECTION

A wealth of literature exists regarding reflection and reflective practice. Much of this has been built around, or developed from, the established theories and models of reflection outlined in Table 1.1. You will find it useful to read literature relating to all of the models presented in this table, three of which are discussed below.

Table 1.1 Reflective practice: examples of some of the key theorists

Theorist	Year	Characteristics of model
Jennifer Moon	2006	Progression from description to more critical reflection of events
Donald Schön	2002	Reflecting in action and on action
Johns	1995	Using a framework of five cue questions
Gibbs	1988	Learning by doing
Stephen Brookfield	1985	Reflecting through four different lenses
David Kolb	1984	Cyclical experiential learning model
Chris Argyris and Donald Schön	1978	Single- and double-loop learning
John Dewey (infed)	1933	Active, persistent and careful consideration of any belief or knowledge; challenging those beliefs and that knowledge

Reflection *in* and *on* action

The ability to reflect *in* action and also *on* action is one of the defining characteristics of professional practice (Schön, 2002). Reflecting *in* action (ie while you are actually doing something) may be related to the operational requirements of your classroom practice (for example, managing an activity regarding children's understanding of complex sentences that is not going as well as anticipated). Reflecting *on* action (ie reflecting after an activity or event) may be related to post-lesson consideration about what went well (regarding the activity relating to complex sentences), why it went well and what could have been done better.

Question

What is reflection in action?

Answer

Reflecting on your actions during an experience.

Question

What is reflection on action?

Answer

Reflecting on your actions after an experience.

Schön (2002) suggests that effective reflection needs the involvement of another person who is able to ask you appropriate questions so that your thoughts are not continually driven by espoused theories or theories in use. Espoused theories are the ones that you think that you use, whereas theories in use are the ones that actually align with what you actually do (ie what you think you do and what you actually do may not be the same thing).

Reflecting about your attitudes, beliefs and values requires what Argyris and Schön (1978) call a process of single- or double-loop learning. They contend that the process of single-loop learning (looking at your attitudes, beliefs and values) controls the variables which inform your actions, whereas double-loop learning necessitates you questioning these variables through a process of meta-cognition. Double-loop learning can lead to a change in your thinking and consequently your actions and approaches to future situations.

Activity

Do some research and see what recent literature you can find about single- and double-loop learning.

Case study

Ron's views on learning

Due to his own experiences during his school days as well as his observations of some of the teachers that he has worked with, Ron believes that nature provides each person with a finite, if individual, capacity to learn. He also thinks that the ability to achieve goals within this finite capacity is influenced by a child's background and that children from the poorest backgrounds are destined for low-level qualifications, low-level unskilled employment or even no employment at all. He likes all of the children in his classes and they like him, partly because he believes in praising and rewarding them as much as possible according to his expectations of each child.

Questions

○ Do you think that Ron is doing the right thing by praising and rewarding children according to his expectations of them?

○ Do you think, like Ron, that children have a finite capacity to learn?

○ What strategies might Ron adopt in order to challenge his current thinking?

Answers

Ron's viewpoint is based on his own experiences as a schoolchild and as an observer of some other teachers. While pre-held views are not necessarily wrong, it is still important to review and evaluate them, especially as new research and literature emerges. In this case study, Ron does need to reflect on the reasons for his beliefs. Importantly, he needs to consider what might happen if he challenged his current thinking; if, for example, he asked himself whether children (and adults) might have an indefinite capacity to learn. Ofsted (2013, pp 3–4) contends that:

poverty of expectation is a greater problem ... and bears harder on educational achievement than material poverty.

In order for Ron to challenge his current beliefs, he needs to seek the views of others. He could do this by speaking with and observing outstanding teachers. He could read literature relating to children's capacity to learn and he could also keep up to date with journal articles and policy reports that are relevant to his area of work (eg *The Unseen Children*, Ofsted, 2013).

> ### Activity
>
> Search for information about children's capacity to learn and/or building children's learning power. You might find research by Guy Claxton a good starting place for this activity.

Use of feedback from others

Knowing when to seek advice and feedback from others (HLTA standard 7 – TDA, 2007, p 38) is crucial to the process of reflection. This, according to Brookfield (1995), can be done by:

○ seeing yourself through your own lens;

○ seeing yourself through your colleagues' lens;

○ seeing yourself through the children's lens;

○ seeing yourself through a theoretical lens.

Your own lens

Like Argyris and Schön (1978), Brookfield (1995) thinks that it is important that you consider the reasons behind your thoughts, ie what assumptions you might be making and how your views might differ if these assumptions were not present. Examining and questioning your assumptions can be a really difficult thing to do. You may not be aware of what they are, or you may not want to let go of views that you have held to be true for most of your life.

Here are some examples of assumptions about children's learning.

○ Children whose first language is not English will find it difficult to learn subjects and topics that are taught in English.

○ Children who are naughty either don't want to or can't learn.

○ Children learn best when praised for their efforts.

Some children may struggle to learn subjects and topics that are taught in English. However, with initial support while they are improving their use and understanding of English, they are just as able as children whose first language is English. In fact,

> *Black African children have now caught up with – and Bangladeshi children have surpassed – the performance of White British children by the end of secondary school. … There is now almost no difference between the GCSE results of children who speak English as their mother tongue and those for whom English is an additional language.*
>
> (Ofsted, 2013, p 4)

Children who are misbehaving might be hungry, cold, bored, under-challenged or have a variety of other reasons for being naughty and not motivated to learn. Furthermore, while praise is important, giving too much praise can become ineffective.

Question

What can you do to challenge your own assumptions?

Answer

You may find it useful to read literature relating to your area of teaching or perhaps managing the behaviour of learners. You may also find it useful to record critical incidents in a journal, or verbally through the use of a digital recorder. Doing this gives you an opportunity to challenge yourself about what you do and why you do it. Whichever route you choose, you should consider the following:

○ what happened;

○ what you would like to change and why;

○ what strategy you need to adopt in order to change the experience for next time.

Your colleagues' lens

Critical reflection can be very difficult to achieve on your own. Discussions with your colleagues and observing others' practice are two ways that can help you see your practice differently.

However, discussions need to be purposeful and held within trusted relationships so that honesty and confidentiality are assured. Examples of purposeful learning conversations might include issues relating to classroom practice, institutional issues or regulatory compliance.

Question

Why might it be useful to listen to the views of others?

Answer

Others' viewpoints can help you to consider:

○ how else you could do something;

○ how and why other people do things;

○ what you might be able to do to make teaching and learning experiences better for you and your learners;

○ a situation or issue from a different perspective.

The children's lens

As well as reflecting and evaluating your practice by considering teaching and learning situations from your own or your colleagues' lens you can, as Brookfield suggests, look at your practice from the perspectives of the children that you support. This can help you to see: *'if they take the meanings that you intend them to do from your teaching lessons'* (Brookfield, 1995, p 30).

> ### Question
>
> How can you gather information from the children that you support that will help you to reflect and to improve your practice?
>
> ### Answer
>
> You could, for example, collect post-lesson feedback from the children. This can be done by the use of a traffic light system, through story-telling, use of sticky notes or by asking the children what (and why) they liked and disliked about the lesson.

A theoretical lens

Reading literature can help you to understand your experiences by naming them in different ways and by providing you with some tools to change your approach (Brookfield, 1995). While, as Brookfield notes, discussions with your peers are useful, an appreciation of theoretical frameworks can provide you with information that enables you to challenge and present an argument to others when appropriate.

> ### Activity
>
> Look at literature relating to different approaches to learning, for example cognitivism and behaviourism, and consider how these could help you to understand how you currently think and act.

> ### Questions
>
> o What have you read recently that has informed your practice or challenged any pre-held assumptions?
>
> o How could Brookfield's four lenses be applied to your professional practice?

Answers

Reading a range of material such as journal articles, recently published books and newspapers as well as listening to documentaries or accessing information via social media are useful ways to keep you informed. Importantly, trying out some of the theories, strategies or hints and tips that you read about relating to your practice can help your development as a reflective practitioner through increasing your knowledge, which can subsequently inform your decision making.

Kolb's experiential learning cycle

Kolb (1984) outlines four significant stages of reflection (Table 1.2). He asserts that it is not necessary to start reflecting at any specific part of the cycle. It may be that you observe an experience before you try it out or that you test out an idea which then provides you with the concrete experience.

Table 1.2 Kolb's experiential learning cycle

Concrete experience	Doing something and/or having an experience
Reflecting	Reflecting about the concrete experience and considering what happened, why it happened and what you might do differently next time
Abstract conceptualisation	Formulating your learning and the conclusions that you arrive at following the reflective process about the original experience so that you can have a different type of experience than you did at the start of this process (ie the concrete experience)
Active experimentation	Testing out your newly formed ideas when the opportunity presents itself

Activity

Search for other approaches to reflection that are similar to Kolb's. A good place to start is with Graham Gibbs' reflective practice model.

THE PURPOSE OF REFLECTION

Reflecting on your practice supports your understanding and ongoing improvement of it; which is essential because of the challenges that are demanded of you as a professional as well as the intrinsic motivation that you will undoubtedly have to want to do the best job that you possibly can do.

In 1999 Hay McBer was commissioned by the Department for Education and Employment (DfEE) to research into what made effective teaching and learning. A significant finding from this research, referreded to in Hay McBer's (2000) report, was the influence and impact of nine factors, relating to the classroom climate, which support effective learning.

Clarity	This is about the purpose of each lesson and how it relates to the broader subject, as well as clarity regarding the aims and objectives of the school.
Order	This is within the classroom, where discipline, order and civilised behaviour are maintained.
Standards	This is about having a clear set of standards as to how children should behave and what each child should do and try to achieve, with a clear focus on higher rather than minimum standards.
Fairness	This is the degree to which there is an absence of favouritism and a consistent link between rewards and recognition in the classroom and actual performance.
Participation	This provides the opportunity for children to participate actively in the class by discussion, questioning, group work, presentation to the class, giving out materials, and other similar activities.
Support	This ensures that children feel emotionally supported in the classroom so that they are willing to try new things and learn from mistakes.
Safety	This is the degree to which the classroom is a safe place, where children are not at risk from emotional or physical bullying or other fear-arousing factors.
Interest	This is the feeling that the classroom is an interesting and exciting place to be, where children feel stimulated to learn.
Environment	This is the feeling that the classroom is a comfortable, well-organised, clean and attractive physical environment.

Activity

Read the factors from the Hay McBer (2000) report above and consider the following questions:

○ What do you currently do regarding each of these factors?

○ How could you improve your practice and each child's learning experience in relation to each of these nine factors?

Reflecting on your practice and making necessary changes in relation to classroom disruption can help you to maximise opportunities for children to engage in learning as well as raise their levels of motivation to succeed. Improving your practice can also help you to manage or alleviate stress because a lack of reflection on practice can lead to *'anxiety, frustration, and often failure'* (Knowles, 1975, p 15).

APPLICATION OF REFLECTION

Reflection can take place at any time, but you need to consider when it is likely to be most effective for you. If possible, you should reflect and evaluate your practice at the end of each lesson so that you can make informed decisions about any necessary changes required to improve any follow-up or similar lesson.

As well as reflecting *on* action there will be times when you reflect *in* action; when you make an instant decision to amend or change your plans or to perhaps intervene in an incident. The consistent application of reflection on your practice will develop your ability to make appropriate decisions and to take appropriate actions.

Reflection is necessary following a critical incident (which might be either positive or negative). However, doing this immediately following an incident may not be possible. If there is time to make a few notes or to jot down a few initial thoughts, that would be useful, but this will not always be possible, with lessons often being back to back and other duties needing to be completed. However, the ability to critically reflect can be improved by gathering together as much information as possible for when you do have the time. Doing this will help you to make informed decisions that are as devoid of espoused theories and assumptions as possible as well as being grounded in whatever data is available. Reflection should occur as soon as is realistically possible after the incident or an event.

Question

When do you currently engage in reflection of your practice?

Answer

You might have said that you reflect when you are on your way home from work or when you get home and are sitting in a relaxing chair with a cup of tea or coffee. What's important is that you do reflect and that how and where you do this is right for you. The time of day as well as your emotional state of mind can make a difference to your engagement in reflection and any decisions you make regarding future actions.

WHAT IS CPPD?

Improving your own knowledge and practice (HLTA standard 7 – TDA, 2007, p 38) is an essential part of the process of reflection. Consideration of your continuing personal and professional development (CPPD) needs can help you to develop a suitable plan of action for achieving any goals, including strategies for changes in your behaviour, which you have set.

CPPD can take many forms, for example, reading this book is a form of CPPD. CPPD can involve formal or informal approaches to learning and updating your skills. It can be directly related to developing your skills in the classroom or your longer-term career progression.

Question

Why should you regularly engage in CPPD?

Answer

Whether you are new to your role or have many years' experience, you need to reflect upon your current situation and ability to do your job efficiently and effectively as *'length of experience does not automatically confer insight and wisdom'* (Brookfield, 1995).

Identifying areas for improvement

Reflecting on your current roles and responsibilities and carrying out a skills audit to detect any developmental needs can be a good start to identifying any areas for improvement. Completing the skills audit in Table 1.3 can help you to do this, as can reviewing any recent appraisals that you may have had.

Table 1.3 Skills self-audit template
Tick a box for how you feel about each skill: 1 = confident; 2 = need a brush-up;
3 = need support

Skills, knowledge and attributes	1	2	3	Evidence to support your response	Action
I am up to date with job-related legislation and regulatory requirements.					
I carry out the tasks required of me in my job role to a high standard.					
I reference sources of information correctly.					
I am able to skim and scan reading materials.					
I am able to critically analyse academic reading.					
I can take useful notes from my reading.					
I manage my time between study, work and home effectively.					
I can write coherently and cohesively, in paragraphs.					
I use grammar and punctuation correctly in assignments.					
I am able to spell specialist words and can employ spelling techniques.					
I can proofread my work effectively.					

Adapted from: Machin et al (2013, p 161).

As part of the reflective process, look carefully at those skills where you have judged yourself to be a 3 and ask yourself:

○   What is the reason for this?

○   Is development of the skill really necessary (will I use it)?

Sometimes your time can be better used by getting even better at what you are already good at rather than spending time developing skills that you are not good at and will rarely use. Engaging in critical reflection about this and challenging assumptions can be really beneficial to you.

Following completion of the audit you may find it useful to discuss your answers with a friend or a colleague. The audit is a tool to help you with your reflections regarding potential CPPD requirements and, as noted earlier in this chapter, if you don't act on your reflections, nothing is likely to change. You may have heard the adage that is often attributed to Benjamin Franklin: *'fail to plan, plan to fail.'*

Once you have identified what you want or need to achieve, you should devise an action plan (an example of an action plan is provided in Table 1.4). Whether you use this template or devise one of your own, remember to:

○   use SMART (specific, measurable, attainable, realistic, timed) targets that can help you to achieve your goals;

○   review and reflect on the impact of your actions on your practice and on you as a person.

Table 1.4 An example of an action plan

ACTION PLAN			
General	**Specific**	**Strategy**	**By when**
Professional roles and responsibilities	Update on latest Ofsted framework	Read Ofsted framework and connected literature. Attend Ofsted workshop	
Skill development	Use and understanding of learning support technology	In-house training event	
Lesson preparation and delivery	Lesson planning to improve children's behaviour	Discussion and peer observation of/with colleagues. Attend conferences and workshops	
	Improving levels of literacy	Read articles about independent learning/building learning power	
Academic development	Referencing and writing at appropriate level	Private study through study skills books/online resources. Attend study skills workshops offered at university/college	

STUDY SKILLS

Some of the skills listed in the self-audit template (Table 1.3) are considered below.

Time-management skills

You will no doubt have many demands on your time, and prioritising these is essential in order to manage your workload efficiently and effectively. You may find it useful to use one or more of the time-management tools that are available, as detailed in Table 1.5.

Table 1.5 Examples of time-management tools

Productivity apps	Give you regular updates about how you spend your time
Project manager	Keeps track of all your on-the-go projects
Electronic calendar/diary/notebook	Enter details about your meetings and events; no more lost scraps of paper
Paper-based calendar/diary/notebook	A resource for note taking and recording events and meetings

You should consider carefully which, if any, of these tools you would actually use, as the utility of these, or any other tools and strategies, depends on how effective you are at using them. All of them will require you to input some initial information.

Another way of developing your time-management skills is to analyse how much time you spend on various activities over the course of a day or a week; knowing this will help you when you are looking at strategies to improve your use of time.

Activity

Divide the day into one-hour segments and use a colour-coding system to decide what time is spent on work, home commitments, travelling, college time, personal studying and other categories specific to your situation. The object of this activity is to get a general idea of how you spend your time and whether you can find *gaps* in your time. The art of time management is to use the short *gaps* profitably because *gap time* accumulates into hours over the course of a week.

Prioritise your tasks

Prioritising which tasks to do first can improve your use of time. Make a list of the tasks that you think you need to do, considering both your longer-term goals and your daily tasks. Ask yourself the following questions.

○ What is the purpose of doing the task?

○ What must be done today (but ask yourself why, as you may be making assumptions based on your current mental models)?

o   Of the jobs that must be done today, which are the most important?

o   How long will each of these tasks realistically take?

You can then put your tasks into the following categories:

o   urgent, must do;

o   important, want to do;

o   not urgent or important but would like to do;

o   can wait.

Importantly, keep to the tasks that you are going to do and don't get distracted by incoming phone calls and emails. However, do take breaks, regular meals and sufficient exercise.

Finally, keep in mind a clear purpose and understand the opportunity cost, ie the cost of what you have given up in order to do the chosen job (Thompson and Machin, 2009, p 225).

Activity

o   Do you easily get sidetracked?

o   Do you drop what you are doing as soon as someone else asks you to do something?

o   Do you hop from task to task?

If you have answered yes to any of the above questions, consider how you can change your actions and manage your time more efficiently. For example, keep a record of what you do during one week and then look at ways in which you could do things differently.

Skimming and scanning

Skimming and scanning are useful skills for you and your pupils! They should not be seen as short cuts that lead to superficial learning. They are time-efficient ways to find information from several sources, after which you can choose to do more in-depth reading as required.

o   Skimming is looking quickly over a piece of text to get the general meaning of it.

o   Scanning is looking quickly over a piece of text to locate a specific piece of information.

How to skim

When you skim for information you should:

o   read the title, abstract, sub-headings and summaries;

o   look at the diagrams, illustrations, tables and charts;

o   read the first and last paragraph;

o   read the first sentence of each paragraph;

o   skim-read the rest of the text;

o   make sure you understand the meaning and context of what you are reading.

How to scan

When you scan for information you should:

o   ensure you are using a reliable source;

o   have a clear purpose and idea about what you want to find;

o   home in on key words or phrases.

Assignment writing

During your studies you are likely to be asked to complete written essays, reports and presentations. Your tutor should give you information about the format required for these, although the following standard essay structure is an easy one to follow.

o   *Introduction* – tell your reader what question you will be answering or what you will be addressing; say how you will go about it and, if necessary, define any specialist terms.

o   *Main body* – there should be one main point within each paragraph. Each paragraph should address the question and group ideas and themes together, but there do need to be links between the paragraphs. A good way to do this is to think of each paragraph as if it were a mini essay on its own. Open with an introductory sentence outlining what the paragraph is going to be about and finish with a sentence that links it to the following paragraph.

o   *Summary and conclusion* – summarise what you have written, come to a conclusion, and show how it answers the question; never add new information to a summary or conclusion.

(Adapted from Machin, Hindmarch, Murray and Richardson, 2013, p 169)

Referencing

Throughout your studies you will need to use a system of referencing. It is important to identify and credit the work of authors as well as to provide evidence of what has informed your ideas. Readers of your work may want to explore the topic further and refer to the references that you have used. Furthermore, it is now common for primary school children to gather information from the internet and it is important that you are able to give them some basic information about the importance of referencing.

A reference list contains details of all the sources that you have used or cited within your text (as opposed to a bibliography, which is a list of all of the sources that you have used to inform you about the topic but which have not been directly included within the text).

One of the most popular models of referencing is the Harvard system, which originates from Harvard University in America.

In-text referencing

If you have paraphrased information in your own words you still need to source the information, but you don't usually need to include the page number. If it is a direct quote you must include the page number/s and use quotation marks. Citations can flow within the text or can be noted in brackets after the appropriate text.

> Testing children's achievement is necessary (Smith, 2003).
> Smith (2003, p 69) considers that 'all children should be tested'.

If the source to which you refer has two authors, then both names should be given. If the source to which you refer is by three or more authors, all three names should be mentioned in the first instance and then any subsequent mention should have the name of the first author followed by et al (Latin for *and others*).

> All children should be tested (Smith, Jones and Myatt, 2003, p 69).
> All children should be tested (Smith et al, 2003, p 69).

Compiling a reference list

If you look at the end of this chapter, or any of the others in this book, you will find examples of Harvard-style reference lists. Each reference that's used should be recorded on a separate line and in alphabetical order using the following format, or a similar one. (It's always a good idea to check out any specific layout requirements with the institution where you are studying as there are many variations of this approach.)

Books

○ author's (or editor's) name/s, surname first, followed by initials;

○ the year the book was published, in brackets. If more than one book by the same author is cited, these should be listed in date order. Where there is work by the same author published in the same year add a suffix to the date, eg (1996a) (1996b);

○ the title of the book (usually in italics);

○ edition number, if more than one version has been published;

○ where the book was published;

○ the publisher's name.

> Machin, L., Hindmarch, D., Murray, S. and Richardson, T. (2014) *A Complete Guide to the Level 5 Diploma in Education and Training*. Northwich: Critical Publishing.

Note: if the reference above was cited in another author's work it would be:

Machin, L., Hindmarch, D., Murray, S. and Richardson, T. (2014) *A Complete Guide to the Level 5 Diploma in Education and Training*. Northwich, Critical Publishing, cited in Davies C. (2014) *Education and Training*. Oxford: Hill Publishers.

Journal articles

○ the author's name/s, surname first, followed by initials;

○ the year the article was published, in brackets;

○ the title of the article;

○ the title of the journal (in italics);

○ any other appropriate information, eg the volume and issue number;

○ the page number/s of the article in the journal.

Smith, C. (1989) Teaching the Teachers, *Journal of Teaching and Learning*, Vol 29: 23–56.

The internet

○ author's name/s if known;

○ the year the article was published, in brackets;

○ the title of the article if known;

○ the full URL address;

○ the date you accessed the source [inside square brackets].

Jones A. (2003) *Referencing*. [online] Available at: www.ref.co.uk/referencesys. html [accessed July 2014].

Question

In which order should references be presented in the Harvard system?

○ alphabetical order by author?

○ alphabetical order by title?

○ date order?

○ the order in which they have been used within the text?

Answer

References should be positioned in alphabetical order by author surname.

Grammar, sentences and punctuation

Grammar is the structural foundation of our ability to express ourselves. It [grammar] can help everyone – not only teachers of English, but teachers of anything, for all teaching is ultimately a matter of getting to grips with meaning.

(Crystal, 2004, p 20)

In order to avoid ambiguity and to ensure that the information that you want to convey is clear, it is important that all your written work is grammatically coherent. This includes any resources that you prepare, report writing that you do and work submitted for CPPD.

Problem nouns

If you are referring to something *specific* (a proper noun), the general rule is to use a capital letter. If you are referring to something that is *one of many* (a common noun), then the general rule is not to use a capital letter. For example:

> I went to Shrewsbury yesterday to watch the cricket.

In the example above, *Shrewsbury* (a specific place) is a proper noun and *cricket* (a general term for a game) is a common noun.

Problem pronouns

A pronoun can replace a noun in a sentence to avoid repetition, for example *she* or *they*. However, problems can arise when it is not clear to whom or what the pronoun is referring:

> Gloria asked Olwen about the meeting later that day; she thought it was at 3pm.

In this example, the reader does not know if it was Gloria or Olwen who thought the meeting was at 3pm. The sentence either needs to be rewritten to avoid this ambiguity or the pronoun needs to be replaced with the correct proper noun.

Problem verbs

Verbs are action words like *walk* or *teach*. Problems can arise in choosing whether to use the active or passive voice. The active voice is when the subject of the sentence performs the action. The passive voice is when the action is done to the subject, eg.

> I taught Ashraf. (*I* performed the action)
>
> Ashraf was taught by me. (Ashraf is the subject and the receiver of the action)

Academic writing tends to use the passive voice because it makes the writing appear more objective and it helps with eliminating *I* from the writing (Machin et al, 2013). However, when reflecting and writing about your own practice, it might be more appropriate to use the active voice, so ask your tutor about which approach to use.

Common spelling errors and homophones

Nowadays, spell-checking features or applications are likely to be available on any software you use to create documents. Remember, though, to make sure that these are set for UK rather than American English. Even with the use of a spell-checker, mistakes can, and do, occur and it is important that you proofread your work thoroughly.

A spell-checker won't pick up words that are spelt right but used incorrectly. If you don't already have a dictionary, consider investing in one so that you can look up the spellings and definitions of any words that you are unsure of. Alternatively, you can look up the meanings of words on the internet. Words that sound the same but are spelt differently and have different meanings are call homophones, for example *right* and *write, dear* and *deer.*

Question

Can you think of at least six homophones?

Answer

If you search for homophones on the internet you will find that there are over 200 homophones (see Table 1.6 for a few examples).

Table 1.6 Examples of homophones

their	there	they're
your	you're	
hare	hair	
air	heir	
scene	seen	
pear	pare	pair
stationery	stationary	
to	too	two

ie or *ei*?

You have probably heard of the spelling rule:

> *i before e except after c*

This is a useful rule to know but it only applies to words where it represents an 'ee' sound, and there are many exceptions to it.

Question

Can you think of any exceptions to the *i before e except after c* rule?

Answer

Common exceptions are *weird* and *seize* (for *ei* when the rule would predict *ie*) and *species* and *fancied* (for *ie* where the rule would predict *ei*).

Use of suffixes

A suffix is an addition at the end of a root word, for example: *able, ance, ing, ment, ly*. As a general rule, this does not alter the spelling of the root word. An exception to this is if the root word ends in a vowel and the suffix starts with a vowel. When this happens the vowel from the root word is (generally) removed.

Punctuation

The colon and semicolon

A colon is represented by two dots (:) and is generally used to introduce a list of items. For example, *teaching assistants need to know about the following policies: bullying, harassment, safeguarding*. A semicolon is represented by a dot and a comma (;) and is generally used to join two clauses together that, on their own, could be independent sentences. For example, *Sally went shopping on Saturday; she bought a new bag*.

Another use of the semicolon is to join two clauses using a transition such as *however, therefore*, or *on the other hand* (Machin et al, 2013). For example: *The sun has been shining all day; however, rain is expected tomorrow.*

Apostrophes

There are two reasons for using an apostrophe.

1. For contracted words, eg *do not* becomes *don't*.

2. To show possession. The word requiring the apostrophe will be a noun (Machin, 2009). Whether an apostrophe is placed before or after the final s depends upon whether the word is singular or plural, eg *the girl's bike* is the bike belonging to one girl, and *the girls' bikes* are the bikes belonging to many girls. If a word is already plural before an s is added, eg *children*, then the apostrophe generally needs to be placed before the s – *children's learning*.

It's or *its*?

○   *It's* is a contraction of *it is* or *it has*. If a sentence does not make sense if *it's* is expanded to *it is* or *it has* then it does not have an apostrophe. *It's lovely weather for the children's outing* can be expanded to *It is lovely weather …*

○   *Its* (no apostrophe) is possessive – it owns something, eg *The dog chased its tail.*

Question

What are two main uses of the apostrophe?

Answer

When words are contracted and in order to show possession of something.

Check your understanding

1. Write one sentence that defines reflection.

2. Give two benefits of engaging in reflection.

3. Explain why reflecting about your practice is important.

4. What questions could you ask yourself when you start to reflect?

5. What factors do you think help to create a positive classroom climate?

6. Look at the questions below and circle the correct answer.

    A. et al means:

        a. with others;

        b. and others;

        c. no others.

    B. A quotation within the text is usually referenced by:

        a. author, book/www address, date, page;

        b. author, date, page;

        c. author, page, date.

    C. When referencing the internet (within the reference list) you should

        a. include the date of publication;

        b. include the date accessed;

        c. include the date of publication and the date accessed.

    D. When referencing the internet (within the reference list) you should

        a. include all of the URL address;

        b. include the main URL address without extensions;

        c. include the URL address, with author, title
            of article and dates (if available).

> ▶▶ **TAKING IT FURTHER**
>
> In addition to the literature noted in this chapter you may find the following of interest.
>
> Brookfield, S (2012) *Teaching for Critical Thinking: Tools and Techniques to Help Learners Question Their Assumptions*. California: Jossey-Bass.
>
> Kohn, A (1999) *Punished by Rewards: The Trouble with Gold Stars, Incentive Plans, A's, Praise, and Other Bribes*. Boston, MA: Houghton Mifflin.
>
> McMillan, K and Weyers, J (2007) *How to Write Essays and Assignments*. Harlow: Pearson Education.
>
> Truss, L (2003) *Eats Shoots and Leaves: The Zero Tolerance Approach to Punctuation*. London: Profile Books.

REFERENCES

Argyris, C and Schön, D (1978) *Organizational Learning: A Theory of Action Perspective*. Reading, MA: Addison-Wesley.

Brookfield, S (1995) *Becoming a Critically Reflective Teacher*. California: Jossey-Bass.

Crystal, D (2004) In Word and Deed. *TES*, 30 April. [online] Available at: www.tes.co.uk/article.aspx?storycode=393984 (accessed November 2014).

Hay McBer (2000) *Research into Teacher Effectiveness: A Model of Teacher Effectiveness*. (DfEE Research Report 216) London: DfEE

Knowles, M (1975) *Self-Directed Learning: A Guide for Learners and Teachers*. California: Jossey-Bass.

Kolb, D (1984) *Experiential Learning – Experience as the Source of Learning and Development*. New Jersey: Prentice-Hall.

Machin, L (2009) *The Minimum Core for Language and Literacy, Audit and Test*. Exeter: Learning Matters.

Machin, L, Hindmarch, D, Murray, S and Richardson, T (2013) *The Complete Guide to the Level 4 Certificate in Education and Training*. Northwich: Critical Publishing.

Mezirow, J (1991) *Transformative Dimensions of Adult Learning*. California: Jossey-Bass.

Moon, J (2006) *Reflection in Learning and Professional Development*. Oxon: Routledge.

Ofsted (2013) *The Unseen Children*. HMCI's (Sir Michael Wilshaw's) speech, June 2013.

Schön, D (2002) *The Reflective Practitioner*. Aldershot: Ashgate.

Thompson, R and Machin, D (2009) *A Level Business Studies*. London: HarperCollins.

Training and Development Agency for Schools (TDA) (2007) *Higher Level Teaching Assistant Candidate Handbook*. London: TDA. [online] Available at www.education.gov.uk/publications/eOrderingDownload/TDA0420.pdf (accessed August 2014).

2 Education, learning and development

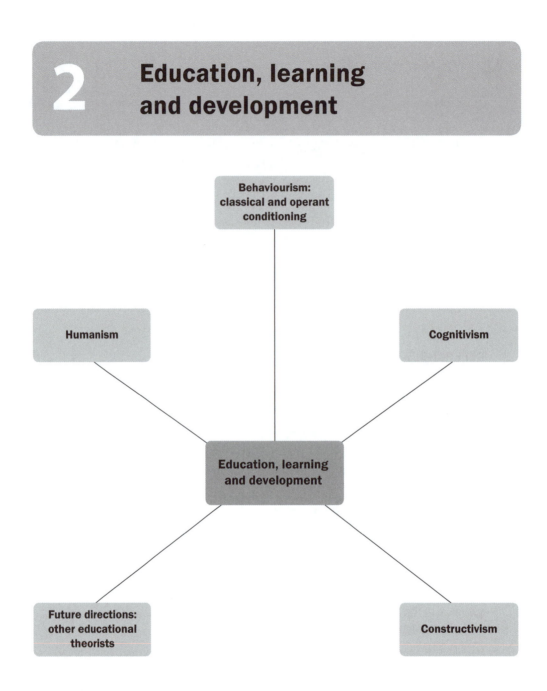

Behaviourism: classical and operant conditioning

Humanism

Cognitivism

Education, learning and development

Future directions: other educational theorists

Constructivism

HLTA STANDARDS

This chapter links to the following HLTA standards (Training and Development Agency for Schools (TDA), 2007, pp 97–98):

1: have high expectations of children and young people with a commitment to helping them fulfil their potential;

3: demonstrate the positive values, attitudes and behaviour they expect from children and young people;

8: understand the key factors that affect children and young people's learning and progress.

INTRODUCTION

This chapter is about theories and the *best* way to learn. There are many 'experts' who know how children learn. You may know some; you may even *be* one! These theories change over time, just like human beings. An expert writing a hundred years ago believed children learned best by following instructions and 'knowing their place'; now the children are the starting point. Such are theories; they will come and go and maybe come back again. That doesn't mean they are wrong. Nor does it mean they are of no use anymore. See what you think.

STARTING POINT

Think of a child you work with who has caught your attention.

o Why *does* he/she behave like that?

o What makes some children co-operate and others refuse?

o Is it genetic – something inside the child; or is it external – something in the child's environment that 'triggers' certain responses?

BEHAVIOURISM: CLASSICAL AND OPERANT CONDITIONING

As someone once said, the past is a different country. How did people used to learn? The answers are often surprising and give you an insight into how some people used to think, and how some still do. The first *modern* educational theory was *Behaviourism*, which first became popular around a hundred years ago. Behaviourism talked about *cause* and *effect*: you wanted a child to learn something, then you taught them. Debates about the *best* way to teach and learn were in the future.

For example, an arithmetic (mathematics) lesson would be straightforward: teach the children how to do a sum, the children practise the method on harder sums and the children learn. Also with English: teach how the sentence is structured, the children assemble the component parts (words) into sentences, string lots of sentences together (paragraphs), then string lots of paragraphs together (an essay).

Behaviourism is seen as simple and straightforward and has a certain appeal around order and discipline. In what some see as a back-to-basics approach (Bukard, 2010) to learning, one size fitted all, no matter who you were or where you came from. In an oft-quoted passage from the 'father' of behaviourism, John Watson (1878–1958), regardless of income or cultural background you could learn given the correct stimulus. Watson was an American psychologist:

> *Give me a dozen healthy infants, well-formed, and my own specified world to bring them up in and I'll guarantee to take any one at random and train him to become any type of specialist I might select – doctor, lawyer, artist, merchant-chief and, yes, even beggar-man and thief, regardless of his talents, penchants, tendencies, abilities, vocations, and race of his ancestors.*

> (John B Watson, 1930)

Put a child from any background in Eton (fees £30,000 per year) and the same results will be achieved. Watson is the person to quote regarding *classical* conditioning.

The learner's thoughts were irrelevant. Watson stated, *'this is a purely objective experimental branch of natural science … Its theoretical goal is … prediction and control'* (Watson, 1913, p 161). Behaviourism (*behavioural psychology*) is a theory of learning. All behaviours are acquired through conditioning through interaction with the environment. Behaviour can be studied in a systematic and observable manner with no consideration of internal mental states. Only observable behaviours should be studied; internal states such as cognitions, emotions and moods are too subjective. Behaviourism is straightforward to understand:

cause = effect

The cause is the teacher (or the lesson) and the effect is learning. The sentence about the *subjective* experience of the learner is crucial. Behaviourism isn't interested in what the learner *thinks*, only what the learner *does*. Does behaviourism work or is it outdated?

Question

How would you teach the following?

a. key sentences in a foreign language;

b. multiplication (times) tables;

c. children to stop playing and line up for class;

d. children to comply in class and beyond;

e. an actor her lines.

Answer

Ideas include:

a. repetition;

b. drills;

c. a whistle or bell;

d. routines;

e. drill and repetition.

Operant conditioning

B F Skinner (1905–90) developed Watson's ideas and refined them, talking of *operant* conditioning. You will doubtless be introduced to Skinner's rats experiment. Look it up. He talked of reinforcement, which we understand as rewards and sanctions: the carrot or the stick. Think about how your school/workplace praises good behaviour and stops (sanctions) unwanted actions.

Activity

○ Can you add to the following list?

  – smiley face – literal, sticky or electronic – for things you want to praise;

  – sad face for things you want to discourage;

  – 'golden time' or similar rewards.

○ Find your school's behaviour policy and identify any obvious 'cause and effect' principles.

Behaviourism is certainly still applicable. As Smith (2004) mentions, *'systems that reward children for improved attention, learning, accuracy, productivity, and behaviour have particularly powerful effects on their learning rates and spontaneous use of learning strategies'* (Smith, 2004, p 278). Everyone is affected by rewards and punishments. Look around and you may be surprised how much of our world is organised on behaviourist principles.

If Watson is the father of *classical* conditioning, Skinner is the quotable 'expert' on *operant* conditioning: behaviour that is reinforced (*with reinforcers*) tends to be repeated (ie strengthened); behaviour that is not reinforced tends to die out – or be extinguished (ie weakened).

Ivan Pavlov

The above is fine in relation to a snooker ball: you hit it, it moves – cause and effect. But what happens if the subject doesn't *want* to move? The snooker ball has no choice, but any dog owner will tell you how hard it is to shift a stubborn animal. The key is to find out *why* the dog won't co-operate. Ivan Pavlov (1849–1936) said this type of learning involves making an association between a *stimulus* and a *response*. You have probably heard of Pavlov's dogs. In a classic experiment, Russian physiologist Pavlov discovered that repeatedly pairing the sound of a bell with the presentation of food caused dogs to associate the tone itself with food. Once the association was formed, the sound of the bell alone could make the dogs begin to salivate in anticipation of a meal (McLeod, 2007b).

Pavlov argued children learn in much the same way, developing associations between things in their environment and potential consequences. For example, an infant may link the sight of a baby bottle with being fed, or a student may associate the playing of certain music in a classroom with generating a positive mind set (Cherry, 2014b). The word *Pavlovian* has come to describe the process of 'conditioned responses' – desired unthinking outcomes. Critics, however, don't accept that it can be fully applied to humans, who, after all, think for themselves. With any theory, there are strengths and weaknesses – see Table 2.1 for a summary of the strengths and weaknesses of behaviourism.

Table 2.1 Behaviourism: strengths and weaknesses

Behaviourism	
Strengths	**Weaknesses**
It's scientific, clinical and 'teacher proof'. Providing you teach the right stuff, you get the correct results. Behaviourism is based upon observable outcomes (orderly classrooms, exam passes). It is easier to quantify and collect data and information (league tables) when conducting research (good and 'failing' schools). It is simple 'no nonsense' teaching and learning.	It's cold, calculating and distant. Humans are not computers or dogs. It is a one-dimensional approach to understanding human behaviour. Behavioural theories do not account for free will (agency) or internal influences such as moods, thoughts and feelings.
It works. Effective therapeutic techniques such as intensive behavioural intervention, behaviour analysis, token economies (charts, stickers) and discrete-trial training are all rooted in behaviourism. These approaches are often very useful in changing maladaptive or harmful behaviours in both children and adults.	It doesn't work for all. Behaviourism does not account for other types of learning, especially learning that occurs without the use of reinforcement and punishment. What if a learner does not respond to either?
	People and animals are able to adapt their behaviour when new information is introduced, even if a previous behaviour pattern has been established through reinforcement.

Adapted from Cherry (2014b)

Question

Go back to the child you chose in the starter activity. From a *behaviourist* perspective, what could be done?

Answer

o   Find what 'works'. It doesn't matter why those stickers or 'time out' on the tablet works, it just does.

o   Praise; lots of it, and it often seems to work better than punishment.

COGNITIVISM

Cognitivism claims to explain how and why learning happens. It is a theoretical framework for understanding the mind and actions. Unlike behaviourists, cognitivists argued that the *way* people think affects their behaviour and can be examined scientifically. It was an attempt to explain what was occurring *in the mind* during learning. In the past, actions were deemed valid proof that learning had occurred; however, cognitivism wanted more: tasks were analysed and broken down into smaller steps to find the most efficient way of learning. Table 2.2 details some theorists that advocated and developed cognitivism.

Table 2.2 Principal cognitive theorists

Kurt Zadek Lewin (1890–1947)	Lewin developed field theory: learning is the result of changes in cognitive structure. In an early echo of neuroplasticity, Lewin posited that learning actively changed the shape of the brain, enabling more learning. Lewin is also credited with the term 'action research', something you will hear a lot of as you proceed to your degree and beyond.
Robert Mills Gagné (1916–2002)	Gagné developed information-processing theory, which identified eight levels of intellectual skills: signal, stimulus–response, chaining, verbal association, multiple discrimination, concept formation, principle formation and problem solving. In the days of behaviourism, you were either 'bright' or 'dull'. Gagné showed us there is more than one way to be 'able', a concept now generally accepted in the contemporary classroom.
Benjamin Samuel Bloom (1913–1999)	Bloom described the domains of learning. He identified three: cognitive (intellectual), affective (attitudes, values) and psychomotor (motor skills). He also famously developed a hierarchy of 'thinking skills'. Figure 2.1 shows a representation of Bloom's taxonomy applied to the 2014 national curriculum (Chapter 6).

Using Bloom

Starting at the bottom of the hierarchy, you work up to 'higher order' thinking. You can take any statement and 'unpick' it in this way. For example, *Children now have to stay in school until they are 18* (descriptive); *This is a good thing for the individual and society as a generation is schooled more thoroughly* (analysis/ synthesis).

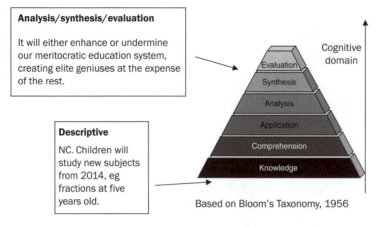

Analysis/synthesis/evaluation

It will either enhance or undermine our meritocratic education system, creating elite geniuses at the expense of the rest.

Descriptive

NC. Children will study new subjects from 2014, eg fractions at five years old.

Cognitive domain

Evaluation

Synthesis

Analysis

Application

Comprehension

Knowledge

Based on Bloom's Taxonomy, 1956

Figure 2.1 Bloom's Taxonomy applied to the 2014 national curriculum.
Based on Bloom's Taxonomy (1956)

It works for any topic. For example, take any premiership football match. Start at the bottom – it is a game – and work to the top – it's an over-hyped commercialised business with illusory and questionable entertainment value or meritocracy in action (Edwards, 2013).

Jean Piaget

Piaget (1896–1980) was one of the most influential cognitive psychologists. He viewed the development of human cognition, or intelligence, as the continual struggle of a very complex organism trying to adapt to a challenging environment. Piaget argued that development *precedes* learning and talked of 'stages' that had to be completed before starting the next one. Piaget has been discredited by some concerned with low expectations (eg McQuillan, 2013) and his 'Western-centric' ideas – meaning it is not wholly applicable *holistically* (Edwards, Hopgood, Rosenberg and Rush, 2000); however, he still remains a starting point for many discussions on child development.

Activity

○ Piaget talked of children being 'ready' to learn. Consider the following issues, thinking about the reasons for and against where you stand. This will influence your teaching approach.

– Primary children in England now have to learn a foreign language (DfE, 2014). Is there any benefit in learning, eg Spanish, before English skills are 'mastered'?

– Mathematics: should we ask children to learn, eg ratios, before times tables are secure?

Criticisms

The cognitive approach is criticised from two 'directions'. It is said to ignore the role biology plays (eg testosterone), and the methodological assumptions are said to lack 'ecological validity', meaning it is entirely subjective: researchers see what they want to see. From a humanist perspective (see below) cognitivism spends too much time in the laboratory controlling variables and not in the 'real world' where people live. For more criticisms see McLeod (2007a).

CONSTRUCTIVISM

Constructivist thinkers realised that things *outside* the classroom affected learning. Social, cultural, and personal factors made a difference to students. It is easy to mock these 'revelations', which seem so much common sense in today's inclusive classrooms, but education had to travel its own journey to get where we are today. The basic tenet of constructivism is that students learn by *doing* rather than *observing*. Children bring prior knowledge into a learning situation in which they must critique and re-evaluate their understanding of it. A good educator will recognise this and 'harness' it: many Key Stage 1 lessons start with 'ourselves' for a reason. Two 'giants' you will hear about are Lev Vygotsky (1896–1934) and Albert Bandura (1925–), who developed learning theories that dealt with those issues.

Vygotsky

Lev Vygotsky developed the *cultural-historical theory*, which took into account the nature of culture and its effect on learning, and the role of social interaction and its impact on the learner (Gredler, 2005). Vygotsky famously talked of zones of proximal development (ZPD): 'pitching' the work – differentiating – slightly in front of the student so they expand their comfort zone and create a new ZPD. This can be seen represented in Figure 2.2.

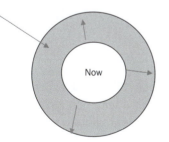

Figure 2.2 Vygotsky's zone of proximal development (ZPD)
(Vygotsky, 1978)

The 'Now' is what the student can learn unaided or 'knows'.

The ZPD is what can be learned with help and is the area of 'potential' where learning takes place. This has to be 'pitched' just right: if the ZPD is too big or too small, there will be no learning.

To ensure development in the ZPD, the guidance received must have certain features.

o   Intersubjectivity – the process whereby two participants who begin a task with different understandings arrive at a shared understanding. This creates a common ground for communication as each partner adjusts to the perspective of the other, eg group or pair work.

o   Scaffolding – adjusting the support offered during a teaching session to fit the child's current level of performance. This captures the form of intervention that occurs as individuals work on tasks such as puzzles and academic assignments, eg show how to structure an essay – students fill in details.

o   Guided participation – a broader concept than scaffolding that refers to shared endeavours between expert and less expert participants. Students learn from each other in mixed-ability groups.

(Adapted from UCD Dublin, nd)

In practice you can see the application in group work around a common task; the level of preparation facilitates or 'scaffolds' learning, and mixed-ability groupings allow stronger students in one subject to guide and 'co-coach' weaker students, to mutual benefit.

Activity

o   Think of a time you have adapted some material to 'stretch' a child. List the processes involved. Start with the material: eg

   –   activity/topic: place value (mathematics);

   –   worksheet (changes made);

   –   ZPD entered/expanded?

o   Did it work? Why/why not?

Bandura

You will probably have heard about Bandura's infamous 'Bobo Doll' experiment. If not, it's worth researching it on the internet. Children copied adults beating a large stuffed toy, and a branch of theory was born. Bandura argued we learn behaviour through social settings such as observations and 'modelling'. Contemporary audiences talk of correct 'role models' (Bandura, 2006).

Most human behavior is learned observationally through modeling: from observing others one forms an idea of how new behaviors are performed, and on later occasions this coded information serves as a guide for action

(Bandura, 1977, p 22)

So a child may simply copy an adult, whether consciously or not. This is perhaps especially true for those for whom an ability to follow verbal instructions is limited: very young children, people with a hearing impairment, people who speak a different language, etc. Two responses are possible: imitation and incidental learning (Research Autism, 2014). Imitation is relatively straightforward: if you're a certain kind of bubbly, extroverted character the children may respond in kind. Incidental responses require more thought. You may, for example, model a respectful attitude by always treating others politely and pleasantly, and this may influence values and attitudes. Or it may not. Bandura recognised that just because something has been learned, it does not mean that it will result in a change in behaviour; it will not necessarily stick. For specific criticisms of Bandura's ethics see Cherry (2014a) at www.psychologyabout.com.

The message is clear: use modelling processes to make a difference at:

o *a cognitive level – helping students to problem-solve;*

o *an attitudinal level – helping students discover the power of intrinsic learning;*

o *a social level – helping students foster a creative and harmonious group climate;*

o *a more 'general' level – helping foster a humane and rational approach to life.*

(Cohen, Manion and Morrison, 2004, p 357)

Bandura also wrote about *self-efficacy* – a sense of *well-being* and a 'can do' attitude. Bandura argued that the education system should focus on teaching students self-regulating efficacy: for example, bolstering their belief that they can not only stay up to date with current technology but also avoid becoming overwhelmed by its continual shift. This will be invaluable as jobs focus more on cognitive abilities as well as flexibility in light of the ever-changing use and applicability of technology in the so-called 'knowledge age' (Moyer, 2011).

Ideally, students will to *want* to learn and Bandura examined forms of internal reward, such as pride, satisfaction and a sense of accomplishment. This emphasis on internal thoughts and cognition helps connect learning theories to cognitive developmental theories. Nowadays we encourage *intrinsic motivation* for independent learning. Bandura's work on phobias is linked to this: building *self-efficacy* – a sense of well-being – is also rooted in Bandura's *social learning theory*.

Jerome Bruner

Discovery Learning (DL) is a method of inquiry-based instruction: it is best for learners to discover any facts and relationships. The learner draws on past experience and existing knowledge to discover 'new truths' to be learned. Children interact with the world by finding out *for themselves*. Bruner (1915–) talked of 'scaffolding' learning whereby adults build a support system – a framework – in which children can grow and develop. An example is structuring an essay, or providing raw tools for a science investigation. Bruner also talked of the *spiral curriculum*, whereby something covered in Year 1 is revisited in greater depth in Year 6.

Question

Find an example of the 'spiral curriculum'. Name a topic begun then revisited in more depth at a later stage.

Answer

An example might include mathematics place value (two digits followed by eight digits) or English adjectives followed by persuasive writing.

The important thing about constructivism as a paradigm is that learning is an *active, constructive process*. The learner is an information constructor. People actively make and shape their own subjective representations of objective reality. New information is linked to prior knowledge, thus mental representations are *subjective*, and discovering that subjectivity is the key to understanding learning processes and *constructing* decent learning opportunities. In plain English: know your learners; find out about them and help them to help themselves.

Question

What does a constructivist classroom look like?

Answer

The main activity in a constructivist classroom is solving problems. Students use inquiry methods to ask questions and investigate a topic, and use a variety of resources to find solutions and answers. As students explore the topic, they draw conclusions, and, as exploration continues, they revisit those conclusions (UCD Dublin, nd). Exploration of questions leads to more questions, and the cycle continues.

Criticisms of constructivism

Critics say that constructivism is elitist and benefits the most extrovert students at the expense of the rest. It has been most successful with children from privileged backgrounds who are fortunate in having outstanding teachers, committed parents and rich home environments. Critics argue that disadvantaged children, lacking such resources, benefit more from more explicit instruction. Further, social constructivism leads to 'group think' where the collaborative aspects of constructivist classrooms tend to produce a 'tyranny of the majority' in which a few students' voices or interpretations dominate the group's conclusions, and dissenting students are forced to conform to the emerging consensus (Tsai, 2001).

HUMANISM

Educational theory has travelled quite a journey. Adults taught, children learned and not much time was spent worrying about those that didn't. This changed, as people realised that some children learned differently than others: being bright no longer sufficed as an explanation. Next, it was realised learning didn't stop and start at the classroom gates: children had their own ideas quite independent of 'official' theories. Enter the last 'great' tradition, although, as we shall see, it is not the end of the story, only the beginning.

Humanists, as the name suggests, put humans and their well-being at the centre. In a nutshell, treat children well and they will learn more. This 'optimistic' view of people is summarised in three central tenets.

o   People are basically good and have an innate need to make themselves and the world better.

o   Personal growth and fulfilment in life are basic human motives.

o   Objective reality is less important than a person's subjective perception and understanding of the world.

(McLeod, 2012)

Two more giants you will hear about are Carl Rogers (1902–87) and Abraham Maslow (1908–70). Maslow's famous hierarchy of needs is perhaps the most often quoted model for explaining motivation. Put Abraham Maslow into a search engine and you'll be treated to an array of triangles and other such diagrams (see Figure 2.3).

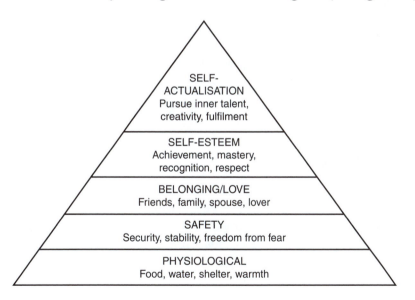

Figure 2.3 Representation of Maslow's Triangle
(Maslow's Hierarchy of Needs, Maslow, 1943)

The central point is one of needs ranging from biological to spiritual and everything in between. At the time of writing, it is planned to give every primary child in England a free meal (BBC News, 2014). This may have something to do with an approaching general election, but the assumption is sound: a cold, hungry child won't learn. Take care of the 'basics' and there's a much better chance learning will take place.

Key, then, to humanist theories are the subjective, conscious experiences of the individual. Thinkers such as Carl Rogers promoted the idea that education needed to move away from being a teacher-centred field in which directed learning was pervasive towards learner-centredness or facilitated learning. The notion of self-directed learning is based on a humanist philosophy where the underlying assumption is that education should focus on the development of the individual.

Thus, from a humanist perspective, learners are seen quite differently from the notion held by more traditional educators of *'empty vessels waiting to be filled with knowledge'*. The essence of humanism is captured in the musings of a tutor:

> *We see learners for what they have to give, their ideas as individuals, and for their life experience and common sense. It breaks down stereotypes of what a learner is in your mind. This essence of personal growth is the core of humanism.*
>
> (Goldgrab, 1992, p 240)

Question

How would a humanist perspective help a child who is non-co-operative?

Answer

Possible answers include:

○ Maslow's triangle – are the 'basics' in place? Is the child fed, warm and clean?

○ lots of unconditional praise;

○ clear directions and expectations.

Criticisms of humanism

Humanistic psychology is often seen as too *subjective*; the importance of individual experience makes it difficult to study and measure humanistic phenomena objectively. How can we objectively tell if someone has learned something? The answer, of course, is that we cannot. We can only rely upon the individual's own assessment of their experience or an *objective* assessment that takes us away from student constructs. For specific criticisms see www.psychologyabout.com.

Table 2.3 Four key theoretical positions

	Behaviourist	**Cognitivist**	**Constructivist (social/ situational)**	**Humanist**
Learning theorists	Thorndike, Pavlov, Watson, Guthrie, Hull, Tolman, Skinner	Koffka, Kohler, Lewin, Piaget, Vygotsky, Bruner Gagné, Chomsky	Dewey, Bandura, Lave and Wenger, Salomon, Bruner	Maslow, Rogers
View of the learning process	Change in behaviour	Internal mental process (including insight, information processing, memory, perception)	Interaction/ observation in social contexts. Movement from the periphery to the centre of a community of practice	A personal act to fulfil potential
Locus of learning	Stimuli in external environment	Internal cognitive structuring	Learning is in relationship between people and environment	Affective and cognitive needs
Purpose in education	Produce behavioural change in desired direction	Develop capacity and skills to learn better	Full participation in communities of practice and utilisation of resources	Become self-actualised, autonomous
Educator role	Arranges environment to elicit desired response	Structures content of learning activity	Works to establish communities of practice in which conversation and participation can occur.	Facilitates development of the whole person
How seen in learning	Behavioural objectives Competency-based education Skill development and training State objectives and break them down into steps Consequences used to reinforce desired behaviour	Cognitive development Intelligence, learning and memory as function of age Learning how to learn Sequence learning key to progression	Socialisation Social participation Associationalism Conversation Problems – realistically complex and personally meaningful. Create group learning activities. Model and guide the knowledge construction process	Pedagogy Self-directed learning

Merriam and Caffarella (1991, 1998)

FUTURE DIRECTIONS: OTHER EDUCATIONAL THEORISTS

It should be clear by now that no single theory can account for learning and development. The secret is to be aware of complementary and contradictory ideas and apply them to your particular circumstances: which theory makes the most sense at the current time, and how likely is it to be superseded in the future? Where will the next educational theory take us? Many theorists take past thinkers as a starting point, which raises the question: are there new theories waiting to be discovered or will old ones simply be 'recycled?

The following are all individuals who defy 'pigeon holing' into one educational theory or another. Are there any educational concepts you recognise or agree with?

John Dewey (1859–1952) was an American philosopher and psychologist who travelled extensively and lectured on the merits of education. He claimed, *'If we teach today's students as we taught yesterday's, we rob them of tomorrow'* (www.deweyproject.net), suggesting nothing is static, certainly not children. He opposed authoritarian methods of education, stating that children should *'not be kept occupied or trained as that did not prepare for a democratic life'* but instead advocated guidance to support a child's development, championing *'varied activities'* rather than a formal curriculum. Lessons on citizenship and 'British values' owe much to the thinking of Dewey, preparing a child 'for life'.

Maria Montessori (1870–1952) was in many ways a remarkable woman. She considered each child an individual with a unique personality. She thought that children needed *protection* from adult intervention, believing that adults *'hindered child development'* by stopping them exploring, discovering and manipulating their own experiences. Children, she argued, should determine their own rate of learning. There are currently 168 accredited *Montessori* schools in the UK (www.montessori.org.uk/msa/find_a_school).

Rudolph Steiner (1861–1925) advocated *'spiritual growth and a holistic education'*. He advocated harnessing *'natural rhythms'*, arguing that children should be given *'no instructions'*; instead the teacher should be a *'role model'*. Crucially, Steiner argued that children should not learn to read until they were 'ready' – not before 7. This concept of when formal schooling should start is not a new one. Schools in Finland do not start formal learning before 7 years of age. There are currently 33 Steiner schools in the UK with 14 at Early Years (www.steinerwaldorf.com).

Guy Claxton (1947–) talks of building learning power (BLP) whereby children's 'learning muscles' are developed in the same way as physical muscles are targeted and improved. According to Claxton, BLP has a *'clear social, moral and philosophical rationale. It puts at the heart of education the development of psychological characteristics that are judged to be of the highest value to young people growing up in a turbulent and demanding world'*. He argues these characteristics are *'capable of being systematically developed'* (www.buildinglearningpower.co.uk). Claxton has a commercial interest in BLP, but has acquired a strong reputation for credibility (Claxton, 2012).

Ken Robinson (1950–) is a world-renowned speaker on educational issues. He argues that current approaches to education are *'stifling some of the most important capacities that young people now need to make their way in the increasingly demanding world of the 21st century – the powers of creative thinking'*. He says:

All children start their school careers with sparkling imaginations, fertile minds, and a willingness to take risks with what they think … most students never get to explore the full range of their abilities and interests … Education is the system that's supposed to develop our natural abilities and enable us to make our way in the world. Instead, it is stifling the individual talents and abilities of too many students and killing their motivation to learn.

(Shepherd, 2009)

In a recent BBC podcast he argued that the *'nineteenth-century model'* of exams and testing should be replaced with humanities and *'much more dancing'* (BBC Radio 4, 2014).

Colin Beard is professor of experiential learning at Sheffield Business School. He believes that we are increasingly working towards a more holistic understanding of learning, and therefore of education. Influenced by Eastern philosophies, he says that this means teachers and lecturers will have to juggle with this complexity alongside day-to-day issues, but sees no contradiction. According to Professor Beard we have to engage not only the

student mind (knowing), but also their emotions (feelings), the actual design of the experience of the learning or education (sensing and doing something), and the two harder elements – the student sense of belonging (to people, community, country, places, natural world, spiritual) and their sense of being (learning to be, someone, a sense of identity, presence, self, psyche, etc.

(Beard, 2014)

A truly comprehensive experience!

CONCLUSION

There are many others who could, and maybe should, have been mentioned. John Bowlby, Noam Chomsky, Howard Gardner and Spencer Kagan are just four who offer vital contributions to how learning happens and possible ways forward. A useful starting point to discover more is *Learning-Theories.com*. However, more authoritative sources will be required for referencing. Similarly, Hugh Gash (2014) has an excellent bank of references to discover more. The important point to remember is that theories, like people, are not static and are continually being developed and adapted.

 Check your understanding

1. Reflect on a lesson you have been involved in. What theories could you see evidence of?

2. How do you see these theories? Are they 'stuck in time' or do they have any value today?

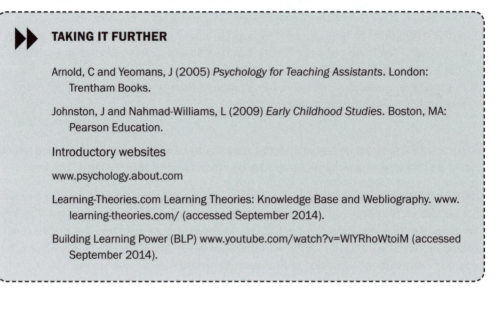

REFERENCES

Bandura, A (1977) *Social Learning Theory*. New York: General Learning Press.

Bandura, A (2006) Autobiography. [online] Available at: www.uky.edu/~eushe2/Bandura/BanduraAutobiography2007.html (accessed August 2014).

BBC News (2014) Nick Clegg: 'Free school meals improve performance', September 2014. [online] Available at: www.bbc.co.uk/news/uk-politics-29026687 (accessed September 2014).

BBC Radio 4 (2014) *The Educators' Ken Robinson*. BBC Podcast 1 September. [online] Available at: www.bbc.co.uk/programmes/b04d4nvv (accessed 11 November 2014).

Beard, C (2014) Positive Emotions. [online] Available at: http://colinbeard.co.uk/2014/06/positive-emotions-passionate-scholarship-and-student-transformation/ (accessed September 2014).

Bloom's Taxonomy (1956). [online] Available at: www.businessballs.com/bloomstaxonomyoflearningdomains.htm (accessed September 2014).

Burkard, T (2010) The Special Needs Industry Is a Gigantic Con. What Pupils Really Need Is to Be Taught Properly, *Mail Online*. [online] Available at: www.dailymail.co.uk/debate/article-1312124/special-needs-industry-what-pupils-need-taught-properly.html (accessed September 2014).

Cherry, K (2014a) [online] Avaliable at: http://psychology.about.com/od/classicpsychologystudies/a/bobo-doll-experiment.htm (accessed September 2014).

Cherry, K (2014b) What Is Behaviourism? [online] Available at: http://psychology.about.com/od/behaviouralpsychology/f/behaviourism.htm (accessed September 2014).

Claxton, G (2012) [online] Avaliable at: www.buildinglearningpower.co.uk/ (accessed September 2014).

Cohen, L, Manion, L and Morrison, K (2004) *A Guide to Teaching Practice* (5th edn). London: Routledge Falmer.

Dewey, J (2014) *The John Dewey Project*. [online] Available at: www.deweyproject.net/ (accessed September 2014).

DfE (2014) *Primary English Curriculum to 2015: programmes of Study.* [online] Available at: www.gov.uk/government/uploads/system/uploads/attachment_data/file/284162/ Primary_English_curriculum_to_July_2015_RS.pdf (accessed September 2014).

Edwards, L (2013) Red Bull Premiership Sponsorship and Commercialization. *The Telegraph*, 10 Nov. [online] Available at: www.telegraph.co.uk/sport/football/10459627/Red-Bull-putting-their-name-to-a-Premier-League-team-would-be-another-step-in-commercialising-the-sport.html (accessed September 2014).

Edwards, L, Hopgood, J, Rosenberg, K and Rush, K (2000) *Mental Development and Education*. Flinders University. [online] Available at: http://ehlt.flinders.edu.au/ education/DLiT/2000/Piaget/begin.htm (accessed Sept 14).

Eton College (2014) Current Fees. [online] Available at: www.etoncollege.com/currentfees. aspx (accessed September 2014).

Gash, H (2014) Constructing Constructivism. *Constructivist Foundations* 9(3): 302–10. [online] Available at: www.univie.ac.at/constructivism/journal/9/3/302.gash (accessed September 2014).

Goldgrab, S (1992) Activating Student Participation, in Draper, J A and Taylor, M C (eds) *Voices From the Literacy Field Culture Concepts*, pp 240–41. [online] Available at: http:// files.eric.ed.gov/fulltext/ED355343.pdf (accessed September 2014).

Gredler, M E (2005) *Learning and Instruction: Theory into Practice* (5th edn). Upper Saddle River, NJ: Pearson. [online] Available at: http://sgo.sagepub.com/ content/2/4/2158244012462707.full#ref-12 (accessed September 2014).

Maslow, A (1943) *A Theory of Human Motivation*. [online] Available at: http://psychclassics. yorku.ca/Maslow/motivation.htm (accessed September 2014).

McLeod, S A (2007a) Cognitive Psychology. [online] Available at: www.simplypsychology.org/ cognitive.html (accessed September 2014).

McLeod, S A (2007b) Pavlov's Dogs. [online] Available at: www.simplypsychology.org/pavlov. html (accessed October 2014).

McLeod, S A (2012) Humanism. [online] Available at: www.simplypsychology.org/humanistic. html (accessed September 2014).

McQuillan, M (2013) Gove, the Enemy of Promise. *Times Higher Education*, 13 June. [online] Available from: www.timeshighereducation.co.uk/features/gove-the-enemy-of-promise/2004641.article (accessed September 2014).

Merriam, S and Caffarella (1991, 1998) *Learning in Adulthood: A Comprehensive Guide*. San Francisco: Jossey-Bass.

Montessori Media Centre (2014) [online] Avaliable at: www.montessori.org.uk/msa/find_a_ school (accessed September 2014).

Moyer, M (2011) What Is the Future of Knowledge in the Internet Age? *Scientific American*, 29 Nov. [online] Available at: www.scientificamerican.com/article/big-data-future-knowledge-internet-age/ (accessed September 2014).

Psychology.about.com (nd) *History of Humanism* [online] Avaliable at: http://psychology.about.com/od/historyofpsychology/a/hist_humanistic.htm (accessed Sept 2014).

Research Autism (2014) Incidental Teaching and Autism. [online] Available at: www.researchautism.net/autism-interventions/our-evaluations-interventions/89/incidental-teaching-and-autism?print=1 (accessed September 2014).

Shepherd, J (2009) Fertile Minds Need Feeding (Ken Robinson) *The Guardian* 10 February. [online] Available at: www.theguardian.com/education/2009/feb/10/teaching-sats (accessed September 2014).

Smith, C R (2004) *Learning Disabilities: The Interaction of Students and their Environments.* Boston, MA: Allyn & Bacon.

Steiner Waldorf (2014) [online] Avaliable at: www.steinerwaldorf.org/steiner-schools/list-of-schools/ (accessed September 2014).

Training and Development Agency for Schools (TDA) (2007) *Higher Level Teaching Assistant Candidate Handbook.* London: TDA. [online] Available at: www.education.gov.uk/publications/eOrderingDownload/TDA0420.pdf (accessed August 2014).

Tsai, C C (2001) Relationships between student scientific epistemological beliefs and perceptions of constructivist learning environments. *Educational Research*, 42(2): 193–205.

UCD Dublin (nd) Educational Theory: Constructivism and Social Constructivism in the Classroom. [online] Available at: www.ucdoer.ie/index.php/Education_Theory/Constructivism_and_Social_Constructivism_in_the_Classroom (accessed September 2014).

Vygotsky, L S (1978) *Mind in Society: The Development of Higher Psychological Processes.* Cambridge, MA: Harvard University Press.

Watson, J B (1913) Psychology as the Behaviourist Views It. *Psychological Review*, 20: 158–78.

Watson, J B (1930) *Behaviorism*, revised edition. Chicago, IL: University of Chicago Press.

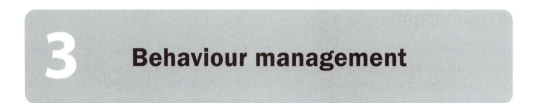

3 Behaviour management

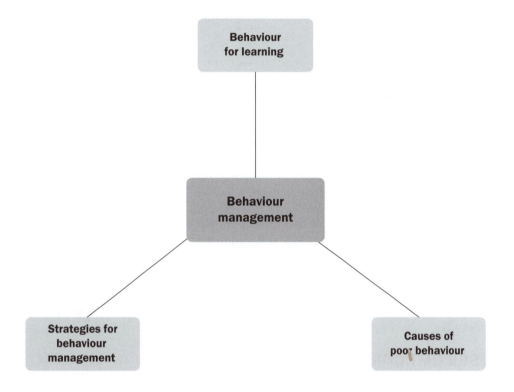

Behaviour
for learning

Behaviour
management

Strategies for
behaviour
management

Causes of
poor behaviour

HLTA STANDARDS

This chapter links to the following HLTA standards (Training and Development Agency for Schools (TDA), 2007a, pp 97–98):

1: have high expectations of children and young people with a commitment to helping them fulfil their potential;

2: establish fair, respectful, trusting, supportive and constructive relationships with children and young people;

3: demonstrate the positive values, attitudes and behaviour they expect from children and young people;

4: communicate effectively and sensitively with children, young people, colleagues, parents and carers;

26: use effective strategies to promote positive behaviour.

INTRODUCTION

This chapter examines the area of behaviour management. In particular, it considers some of the causes of poor behaviour demonstrated by children in schools and how we can encourage learning behaviour. It also reflects on some strategies that can be used to deal with inappropriate behaviour as well as developing techniques to encourage the right behaviour.

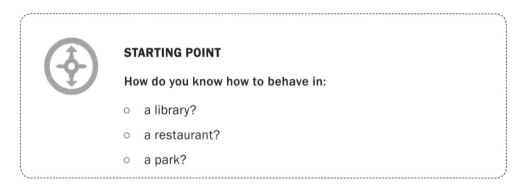

STARTING POINT

How do you know how to behave in:

○ a library?

○ a restaurant?

○ a park?

You generally know how to behave in different situations because, as you grew up, you were told what was expected of you, you had this modelled to you and, as a general rule, people conform to the norms of society. Some people behave in ways that are not seen as acceptable by others and this may be for a range of reasons, such as poor role models or a desire for attention. In childhood we are supposed to learn the behaviours that are socially accepted by society, from our families and schools and nurseries.

CAUSES OF POOR BEHAVIOUR

There are many causes of poor behaviour. Here we will cover the influence of background, personal needs, motivation and self-esteem.

Background

Although, in an ideal world, children grow up in a home where they are loved and supported, with their needs met, this is not always the case. The background of a child is bound to impact on them and this can in turn affect their behaviour. Some children are growing up in challenging circumstances and they don't necessarily leave this behind when they go to school.

Many children are growing up in disadvantaged households. In 2009, *The Protection of Children in England: A Progress Report* by Lord Laming indicated that of approximately 11 million children living in England:

> *200,000 children live in households where there is a known high risk case of domestic abuse and violence;*

> *235,000 are 'children in need' and in receipt of support from a local authority;*

60,000 are looked after by a local authority;

37,000 are the subject of a care order;

29,000 are the subject of a Child Protection Plan.

(Protection of Children in England: Updated Report, Laming, 2009, p 14)

According to Save the Children (2014), 1.6 million children in the UK are living in severe poverty. Children living in poorer quality housing have more than double the chance of being excluded at secondary school (Harker, 2006), with behaviour problems tending to have started when they were younger. Children are also suffering from mental health problems: 850,000 children have been diagnosed, but there will be others attempting to cope without help (Association for Young People's Health, 2013).

Young children deserve to grow up in a stable environment as it is this background that will help them to become well-developed adults. Children will naturally develop some emotions as they grow up, but other more complex ones such as empathy and co-operation need to be taught, and this usually comes from a stable primary caregiver. Poor parenting skills can impact on children's behaviour at school, where they can be seen to lack social skills and respond inappropriately (Department for Education (DfE), 2012). Children who are growing up in violent or poor households are likely to have higher stress levels, which can in turn impair development by reducing motivation, effort and the ability to concentrate, as well as affecting social skills. It can also lead to mental health issues.

Children from poorer backgrounds begin lagging behind educationally from an early age, and by three years old, children growing up in poorer households will be approximately nine months behind children from more affluent homes (Field, 2010). By the end of primary school, pupils who receive free school meals are estimated to be almost three terms behind children from more wealthy backgrounds, and by 16 those same children will achieve 1.7 grades lower at GCSE (Child Poverty Action Group (CPAG), 2014). Although poor academic achievement does not necessarily mean children behave inappropriately at school, it can be a contributing factor as they begin to realise they will not meet the expected milestones. However, it is not always the children from the more disadvantaged backgrounds who cause the issues in schools, as illustrated in the interesting commentary in an article titled 'Bad behaviour in schools "fuelled by over-indulgent parents"' by Graeme Paton in *The Telegraph* (2012).

Individual needs

Children's behaviour is influenced by their individual needs. A significant writer in this area is Maslow, who suggested that we have a range of needs that exist in a hierarchy starting with the most basic of needs, linked to our survival, at the bottom. Maslow indicated that the needs of one level need to be met before it is possible to move to the next level. This is shown in Figure 3.1.

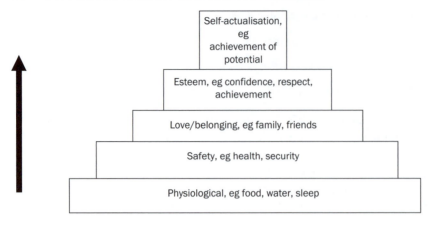

Figure 3.1 Maslow's Hierarchy of Needs

Activity

Consider how each level of Maslow's hierarchy can be applied to your setting.

Motivation

Behavioural problems can also stem from a lack of motivation, so it is important to try and get to know the children you work with. Good behaviour management is about establishing a good relationship between yourself and the children, and finding out what the children are interested in can really help.

For some children, motivation may be intrinsic and they learn because they enjoy learning or see some personal goal in what they do. This may come from being able to select what activity they do or how they do it, or, for older learners, there may be a goal in mind such as university or a career choice. For many children, however, learning involves extrinsic motivation. They are more focused on performance and so are driven by rewards, grades and the threat of failing. Ultimately, both interest and rewards can be powerful motivators and it is the educator's role to find out how to assist children's motivation.

Self-esteem

According to Rae (2010), self-esteem is a big driver in whether children will learn. Self-esteem is about how people value themselves. It is linked to motivation, and a range of issues, such as their relationship with others, achievements and their appearance, will all play their part. Self-concept is linked with self-esteem but it is also about how a person defines themselves and what helps to make them who they are, and factors such as gender, likes and dislikes all have a role in this. We can also talk of the ideal self, which is the person we would like to be, and this is usually assessed through comparison with others. Self-esteem, then, is a combination of our self-concept and our ideal self, and an evaluation of these parts.

For example: I define myself as a parent, a netball player, a teaching assistant, a lover of ice cream, Sally's best friend (self-concept). I want to carry on being/doing all of those things, but I hope to study hard and become a teacher (ideal self). My self-esteem comes from evaluating these things: am I a good parent/friend/TA? Will I manage to pass GCSE mathematics at the third attempt in order to become a teacher?

Low self-esteem can be the result of a distorted evaluation of your self-concept and your ideal self but it may also be a result of bullying or inferiority issues. Low self-esteem can also be caused by an inability to communicate well, which can lead to poorer social relationships. However, we can all suffer from low self-esteem occasionally, when we have a temporary knock-back, but most of us usually have enough good things happening in our lives to bring us round again. In order to develop high self-esteem, children do need to be confident enough to take risks, but this also involves the chance of failure, and children need to be supported through these processes so that they continue to try. Children's self-esteem will grow if they take responsibility for their actions and their actions begin to have some merit. The link between self-esteem and achievement is debated: does high self-esteem improve achievement or is it the other way round? However, what is clear is that children who believe in themselves do better (Rae, 2010).

Question

List some ways that you can adjust your practice to help children with lower self-esteem.

Answer

You might have thought of some of the following:

- specific and genuine praise;
- value their attempts but in an appropriate manner;
- help them develop in areas where they are showing potential;
- set realistic and achievable targets and encourage them to set their own;
- help them to overcome setbacks;
- avoid comparisons;
- allow them to make choices and take responsibility;
- encourage them to do more of what they are good at;
- share success with others including parents;
- highlight successes;
- find ways to show they are valued;
- talk to children about what they like.

Although there is no comprehensive link between these areas and poor behaviour, they have the potential to affect how a child behaves in class. A child with poor self-esteem may believe they cannot achieve and so will fail to engage in the learning. A child who comes to school hungry may act aggressively to others or fail to listen but may well have no comprehension of why. It is the job of the practitioners in schools to attempt to eliminate the impact of as many of the negative background influences as possible.

BEHAVIOUR FOR LEARNING

Encouraging the right behaviour for learning can be as much about the learning environment as anything else. Jensen (2009) stresses the importance of four domains that impact on learning: physical, social, academic and cultural.

> *The school environment influences students so much that the 4 environmental domains become make or break factors in determining students' likelihood to succeed or fail.*

> (p 61)

Failure in the learning environment will significantly affect children's stress levels, feelings of safety, confidence and behaviour, and it is important to make the environment conducive to learning.

The physical environment

The physical space within which children learn can affect behaviour for learning. If the space isn't adequate then behaviour may be affected. A classroom with poor acoustics can make it difficult for children to hear what is going on or they may be competing with noisy radiators or heating/cooling systems. A classroom that is stuffy or too warm will make children less receptive and obtain poorer results. Poor lighting can also play its part in making a classroom less conducive to learning, and natural sunlight has been shown to improve performance significantly. Space is also a key factor that can affect behaviour. Many classrooms are cramped, with poor use of space. If children are all crowded into a small space to change and hang up coats, it is inevitable that there will be issues.

The social environment

Too often we look upon education as an individual act, but we are naturally social creatures, usually preferring to be in groups. Peers can be very powerful, so we need to make sure these peer relationships are focused towards learning in a positive manner. Social learning has been shown to improve well-being and in turn performance. Working in groups can reduce stress, increase self-esteem and lead to better academic performance, all of which can impact positively on behaviour.

The academic environment

The academic climate needs to be managed by the teacher or TA to ensure learning takes place. It is made up of the characteristics of the school, teachers and children and hopefully sends strong messages about the value of a good education. To be successful the academic environment needs to celebrate and affirm learning, engender a long-term ambition in children, make use of school and class routines and traditions, offer variety in the way lessons are presented, and develop children's skills and abilities. All of this helps to maintain children's focus and with it create a greater chance of appropriate behaviour for learning. Consistency and interesting and varied lessons, with planning for clear beginnings and endings, create a more academic environment.

The cultural environment

The children's culture influenced by home and family will impact on their ability and desire to learn but so too will the culture encouraged in the classroom, particularly in relation to success, character and respect. However, children can be influenced by the countercultures that exist, such as apathy instead of success, as some feel that they cannot do well. Classrooms that encourage positive character in the guise of support and encouragement produce more conscientious children who are likely to do better. The counterculture to character is rebellion and rule-breaking, and success reduces this likelihood. We are more likely to respect others who are like us, so it is important to find out about the children and get them to share interests so they realise what they have in common. A counterculture exists when differences are perceived and result in bullying and prejudice; children will not feel safe and cannot thrive and learn well in situations like this.

Office for Standards in Education (Ofsted)

Ofsted plays a large part in assessing whether schools are creating the right environment to encourage behaviour for learning, and, as of 2014, they are able to undertake unannounced inspections of schools where there are concerns regarding behaviour.

Ofsted 2014, *The Framework for School Inspection: Behaviour and Safety of Pupils at School*

This judgement takes account of a range of evidence about behaviour and safety over an extended period. This evidence may contribute to inspectors' evaluation of how well the school promotes pupils' spiritual, moral, social and cultural development.

Inspectors will also consider the behaviour and safety of pupils attending on-site and off-site alternative provision. When evaluating the behaviour and safety of pupils at the school, inspectors will consider:

○ *pupils' attitudes to learning*

○ *pupils' behaviour around the school and in lessons, including the extent of low-level disruption*

○ *pupils' behaviour towards, and respect for, other young people and adults, and their freedom from bullying, harassment, and discrimination*

○   *pupils' attendance and punctuality at school and in lessons*

○   *how well teachers manage the behaviour and expectations of pupils to ensure that all pupils have an equal and fair chance to thrive and learn in an atmosphere of respect and dignity*

○   *the extent to which the school ensures the systematic and consistent management of behaviour*

○   *whether pupils feel safe and their ability to assess and manage risk appropriately and to keep themselves safe*

○   *the extent to which leaders and managers have created a positive ethos in the school.*

(Ofsted 2014 framework, pp 18–19)

Activity

Consider how your school would measure up against these criteria.

STRATEGIES FOR BEHAVIOUR MANAGEMENT

There is no set formula for managing difficult behaviour. However, there are a range of strategies that often work to counter the low-level disruption that can impact on the ability to maintain an environment conducive to learning. The key thing to remember is that poor behaviour will not go away on its own; it will get worse if it is not responded to and will continue to impact on your stress levels and the learning of others.

Policies

Behaviour polices are there to set out clear expectations regarding behaviour in the school and to ensure the value system of the school is clearly laid out. It is a legal responsibility of all schools to produce a school behaviour policy that sets out how it plans to: promote good behaviour, self-discipline and respect; prevent bullying; ensure that children complete the work set; and regulate the children's conduct (Department for Education (DfE), 2014).

Maintained schools are required to publish their policy on the school website and academy schools are strongly advised to do the same. In addition, headteachers are required to remind staff, parents and pupils of the policy once a year. Also, the standard of behaviour expected from pupils should be raised in the home–school agreement that parents are asked to sign. It is vital that there is a consistent approach to behaviour management, supported by strong leadership with co-operation and involvement of staff, parents and children. The DfE (2014) document *Behaviour and Discipline in Schools Advice for Headteachers and School Staff* offers comprehensive guidance for schools on what is expected. Some schools produce a whole-school approach, while others tailor it to key stages so that it can be made more appropriate. Some primary teachers may have their own class policy or rules that have been developed with the children. If you support more than one teacher it is important that you know the school policy and any specific class rules so that you can be consistent with the teacher.

Some simple strategies for effective behaviour management

Much low-level disruption can be managed with a few simple techniques when applied consistently. These include

o   the look;

o   remove the audience of the poor behaviour;

o   ask a direct question to aid refocus;

o   redirect their attention to something else;

o   seating plans;

o   blame the behaviour, not the child;

o   stand in close proximity to the child;

o   remind them of the class rule;

o   reduce unnecessary transitions;

o   a quiet chat;

o   tell, don't ask and add thanks at the end, to indicate compliance is expected;

o   proximity praise to a child nearby who is doing the right thing;

o   humour, but avoid sarcasm and humiliation;

o   reminder of consequences;

o   offer choices – if you don't do ... then ....

A key document offering some sound advice has been published by the DfE (2011), *Getting the Simple Things Right: Charlie Taylor's Behaviour Checklists*. The document offers some effective strategies that, while taking a more holistic view on school behaviour, also provide some focused advice for teachers and TAs.

Getting the simple things right

In the classroom

Know the names and roles of any adults in class.

Meet and greet pupils when they come into the classroom.

Display rules in the class – and ensure that the pupils and staff know what they are.

Display the tariff of sanctions in class.

Have a system in place to follow through with all sanctions.

Display the tariff of rewards in class.

Have a system in place to follow through with all rewards.

Have a visual timetable on the wall.

Follow the school behaviour policy.

Pupils

Know the names of children.

Have a plan for children who are likely to misbehave.

Ensure other adults in the class know the plan.

Understand pupils' special needs.

Teaching

Ensure that all resources are prepared in advance.

Praise the behaviour you want to see more of.

Praise children doing the right thing more than criticising those who are doing the wrong thing (parallel praise).

Differentiate.

Stay calm.

Have clear routines for transitions and for stopping the class.

Teach children the class routines.

Parents

Give feedback to parents about their child's behaviour – let them know about the good days as well as the bad ones.

DfE (2011, p 5)

Activity

What aspects from this list can you find in your school's behaviour policy?

Rewards and sanctions

Most behaviour policies will make use of rewards and sanctions. The aim of rewards and sanctions is to elicit more of the desired behaviour and reduce the inappropriate behaviour, and you should see the link here to the behaviourist theories. According to Cowley (2010), rewards:

o   help encourage both behaviour and work;

o   motivate students to try;

o   encourage us to take a positive approach;

o   can boost children's self-esteem.

A reward may be something as simple as a smile, but tangible rewards work best if they are agreed with the children as being something they value. For example, there is no point offering extra physical exercise (PE) as a whole-class reward if some of the children do not enjoy it. Rewards should be age-specific. For some children, they may need to be private.

Furthermore, Cowley (2010) notes sanctions:

o   encourage children to stay within the boundaries set;

o   clarify the rules.

Sanctions, like rewards, can be quite personal to a class or setting. For example, a threat of no playtime may not be seen as a sanction to some children. A sanction needs to be appropriate and proportionate. Never threaten something you can't deliver. Sanctions are often delivered on a scale and this can be written into the school policy. Rewards should be used more than sanctions as children are likely to respond better to the positive than the negative, and a consistent approach is helpful. Cowley (2010) suggests a ratio of 5:1 in favour of rewards. Remember, inconsistent application of sanctions for bad behaviour or rewards for good behaviour undermines your credibility. And children are less likely to change their behaviour if they feel unfairly treated.

Language

Language is a very powerful tool in behaviour management, but you must get it right. It is far better to use positive language to help tackle and avoid behavioural issues. Language is very effective when offering praise as it can help children feel good about themselves. The TDA (2007b) suggests you should also be clear and specific about what the praise is for, for example, *'Well done, Maya, for writing your name so neatly.'* Language can also be used to get children back on track. Sometimes we need to think carefully about what we say, and the TDA (2007b) suggests trying to make statements positive rather than negative.

Questions

Can you make these negative phrases into something more positive?

1. What a mess you made in the art area.
2. What are you doing skulking in the classroom at playtime?
3. You've made Emily cry.
4. Stop talking over each other.
5. How dare you answer back.

Answers

1. Shall we get the friend you were working with and tidy up the art area now?
2. It is such a lovely day; get yourself outside to enjoy the sunshine.
3. Shall we see if we can make Emily feel better?
4. Shall we take it in turns to speak? Jordan, you go first.
5. I need you to listen very carefully to me.

Non-verbal language is also a positive tool in behaviour management and can often be used to encourage compliance with minimal interruption, for example, a finger on your lips.

Managing difficult situations

Fortunately, behaviour doesn't often escalate into a difficult situation, but knowledge of clear systems and procedures helps if this arises. If children are behaving in a very challenging and difficult way you do need to react quickly. Try to:

- calm things down;
- ensure everyone is safe;
- send for help if needed;
- respond in a way that guides others into more appropriate behaviours.

Activity

- Think about a difficult behavioural situation you came across recently.
    - How did you deal with it and could it have gone better?
    - Did you manage to stay calm, and, if so, how?
    - Did you manage to prevent it getting any worse? If so, how?
    - If it did escalate, what would you do differently next time?

Making a difficult situation worse

The TDA (2007b) suggests you can make a difficult situation much worse by:

o   threatening, particularly with something you cannot carry out;

o   giving children no room for manoeuvre both physically and mentally;

o   shouting, being angry, calling the child names;

o   using threatening or aggressive body language;

o   giving unrealistic ultimatums;

o   taking it too personally;

o   not giving the child time or opportunity to speak;

o   telling the child to calm down or using inappropriate tone of voice.

Making a difficult situation better

The TDA (2007b) suggests you can make a difficult situation better by:

o   remaining calm;

o   being assertive and calmly stating your position;

o   stating what you want to happen;

o   labelling the behaviour, not the child;

o   using a calm voice and neutral language;

o   listening to the child and trying to see their point of view;

o   using humour;

o   avoiding an audience;

o   not standing too close;

o   looking for common ground;

o   keeping options open;

o   giving choices.

Questions

How might you deal with each of these situations?

1. You are running a mixed-year-group mathematics intervention, which is held in a small room off the library. Joshua arrives late after break and appears in a bad mood. He wanders round the room and does not sit down.

2. You are working with a small group of children. For the past few minutes Hayley has not been working and is distracting others on the table and

stopping them from doing their work. When you directly challenge her and ask her to stop distracting others and get back to her work, she stares right at you and says loudly that you can't make her.

Answers

1. There are various techniques that might work. You could distract him by asking him to hand out some resources for you. You could ask a direct question to him about something unrelated to get his attention and take his mind off what has happened. You could offer proximity praise to children who are doing the right thing.

2. This is a tricky situation and it is important to remain calm. You could give her a choice that she either resumes her work or she will need to move away to sit on her own. She may be finding the work difficult so it might be worth ensuring she understands what you have asked of her. You may need to remove the audience and ask her to step away from the group so you can have a quiet word. This will also help her to calm down a little. In addition, the DfE (2014) guidelines suggest that children should be expected to carry out reasonable requests and that you are within your right to make them. This situation would certainly fall into this category.

CONCLUSION

Children's behaviour is complex and many things influence how they behave. Their behaviour does not occur in isolation, either, and other children's moods and your own mood can affect how children will respond. However, most minor misbehaviour can be dealt with by having a good behaviour policy that is applied consistently, and although there can be some very challenging behaviour in schools, on the whole, children will be on task and engaged. For the small minority who struggle significantly with behaving in a way that is acceptable in everyday school life, specific intervention strategies may be needed to ensure inclusion in mainstream settings.

 Check your understanding

1. Recap some of the behaviourist theories. How do they relate to behaviour policies and school behaviour management?

2. Compare your policy to that of another setting. Which is better and why?

> ▶▶ **TAKING IT FURTHER**
>
> DfE (2011) *Getting the Simple Things Right: Charlie Taylor's Behaviour Checklists.* London: DfE.
>
> DfE (2012) *Ensuring Good Behaviour in Schools*. London: DfE.
>
> DfE (2014) *Behaviour and Discipline in Schools: Advice for Headteachers and School Staff February 2014*. London: DfE.
>
> Ofsted (2014) *Unannounced Behaviour Inspections*. Manchester: Crown.

REFERENCES

Association for Young People's Health (2013) *Key Data on Adolescence 2013.* [online] Available at: www.youngpeopleshealth.org.uk/3/resources/17/key-data-on-adolescence/ (accessed August 2014).

Child Poverty Action Group (CPAG) (2014) *The Impact of Poverty.* [online] Available at: www.cpag.org.uk/content/impact-poverty (accessed August 2014).

Cowley, S (2010) *Getting the Buggers to Behave*. London: Continuum.

DfE (2012*) How Is Parenting Style Related to Child Antisocial Behaviour? Preliminary Findings from the Helping Children Achieve Study.* [online] Available at: www.gov.uk/government/uploads/system/uploads/attachment_data/file/197732/DFE-RR185a.pdf (accessed September 2014).

DfE (2014) *Behaviour and Discipline in Schools: Advice for Headteachers and School Staff February 2014.* [online] Available at: www.gov.uk/government/uploads/system/uploads/attachment_data/file/353921/Behaviour_and_Discipline_in_Schools_-_A_guide_for_headteachers_and_school_staff.pdf (accessed August 2014).

Field, F (2010) *The Foundation Years: Preventing Poor Children Becoming Poor Adults.* [online] Available at: www.frankfield.com/campaigns/poverty-and-life-changes.aspx (accessed September 2014).

Harker, L (2006) *Chance of a Lifetime: The Impact of Bad Housing on Children's Lives*. London: Shelter.

Jensen, E (2009) *Fierce Teaching*. California: Corwin Press.

Laming (2009) *The Protection of Children in England: A Progress Report*. London: The Stationary Office. [online] Available at: http://dera.ioe.ac.uk/8646/1/12_03_09_children.pdf (accessed August 2014).

Ofsted (2014) *A Framework for School Inspection*. Manchester: Ofsted.

Paton, G (2012) Bad Behaviour in Schools 'Fuelled by Over-Indulgent Parents'. *The Telegraph*, 30 March. [online] Available at: www.telegraph.co.uk/education/educationnews/9173533/Bad-behaviour-in-schools-fuelled-by-over-indulgent-parents.html (accessed 11 November 2014).

Rae, T (2010) Building Self-Esteem in Students. [online] Available at: www.teachingexpertise. com/e-bulletins/building-self-esteem-students-7785 (accessed August 2014).

Save the Children (2014) *UK Child Poverty.* [online] Available at: www.savethechildren.org. uk/about-us/what-we-do/child-poverty/uk-child-poverty (accessed August 2014).

Training and Development Agency for Schools (TDA) (2007a) *Higher Level Teaching Assistant Candidate Handbook.* London: TDA. [online] Available at: www.education.gov.uk/ publications/eOrderingDownload/TDA0420.pdf (accessed August 2014).

Training and Development Agency for Schools (TDA) (2007b) *Promoting Positive Behaviour: For Teaching Assistant Trainers.* London: TDA.

4 Safeguarding and child protection

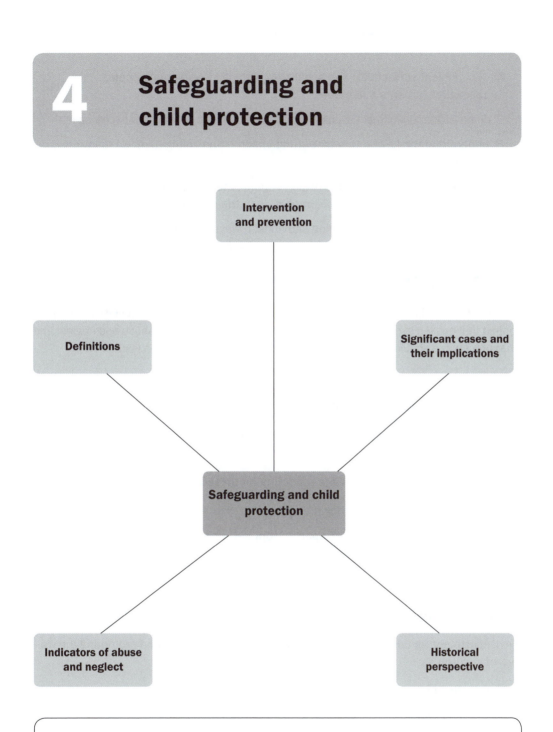

HLTA STANDARDS

This chapter links to the following HLTA standards (Training and Development Agency for Schools (TDA), 2007, pp 96–97):

2: establish fair, respectful, trusting, supportive and constructive relationships with children and young people;

4: communicate effectively and sensitively with children, young people, colleagues, parents and carers;

6: demonstrate commitment to collaborative and co-operative working with colleagues

8: understand the key factors that affect children and young people's learning and progress;

16: know how other frameworks, which support the development and well-being of children and young people, impact upon their practice;

32: organise and manage learning activities in ways that keep learners safe.

INTRODUCTION

This chapter examines the area of safeguarding and child protection, including the historical context that has led to current practices. It outlines how to recognise abuse and neglect and what procedures should be followed upon suspicion of child protection issues.

STARTING POINT

What do you understand by the terms *safeguarding* and *child protection*?

Spend some time reflecting on these concepts.

○ What do they mean to you?

○ How do they apply to your setting?

DEFINITIONS

Safeguarding

The Department for Education (DfE) (2013) defines safeguarding and promoting the welfare of children as:

○ *'protecting children from maltreatment;*

○ *preventing impairment of children's health or development;*

○ *ensuring that children grow up in circumstances consistent with the provision of safe and effective care; and*

○ *taking action to enable all children to have the best outcomes.'*

(DfE, 2013, p 7)

Child protection

Coming under the umbrella of safeguarding is child protection, which is defined as:

part of safeguarding and promoting welfare. This refers to the activity that is undertaken to protect specific children who are suffering, or are likely to suffer, significant harm.

(DfE, 2013 p 85)

The term harm is described in the Children Act 1989 as *'ill-treatment (including sexual abuse and non-physical forms of ill-treatment) or the impairment of health (physical or mental) or development (physical, intellectual, emotional, social or behavioural)'*. The Act does not define what the term significant means and this is left to interpretation should a case reach court, based around the expectations of the health and development of a similar child.

INDICATORS OF ABUSE AND NEGLECT

Abuse is considered to be any kind of maltreatment of children (DfE, 2013), but it is usually categorised into four more specific types:

1. physical abuse;

2. emotional abuse;

3. sexual abuse;

4. neglect.

Question

What do you think is meant by each of the terms listed above?

Answer

Read the following explanations provided by the DfE (2013).

Physical abuse

This may involve hitting, shaking, throwing, poisoning, burning or scalding, drowning, suffocating or otherwise causing physical harm to a child. Physical harm may also be caused when a parent or carer fabricates the symptoms of, or deliberately induces, illness in a child. Some of the signs include such things cigarette burns, bite marks and bruises in areas where you wouldn't expect.

Emotional abuse

This is persistent emotional maltreatment of a child that causes severe and persistent detrimental effects on the child's emotional development. It may involve conveying to a child that they are worthless or unloved, inadequate, or valued only insofar as they meet the needs of another person. It may include not giving the child opportunities to express their views, deliberately silencing them or 'making fun' of what they say or how they communicate. It may feature age or developmentally inappropriate expectations being imposed on children. These may include interactions that are beyond a child's developmental capability, as well as overprotection and limitation of exploration and learning, or preventing the child participating in normal social interaction. It may involve seeing or hearing the ill-treatment of another. It may involve serious bullying, causing children frequently to feel frightened or in danger, or the exploitation or corruption of children. Some of the signs include developmental delays and an inability to form relationships with others.

Sexual abuse

This involves forcing or enticing a child or young person to take part in sexual activities, not necessarily involving violence, whether or not the child is aware of what is happening. The activities may involve physical contact, including assault by penetration (for example, rape or oral sex) or non-penetrative acts such as masturbation, kissing, rubbing and touching outside of clothing. They may also include non-contact activities, such as involving children in looking at, or in the production of, sexual images, watching sexual activities, encouraging children to behave in sexually inappropriate ways, or grooming a child in preparation for abuse. Sexual abuse can be instigated by men and women and other children.

Some of the signs include inappropriate sexual behaviour, excessive masturbation and abdominal pains.

Neglect

Neglect is the persistent failure to meet a child's basic physical and/or psychological needs, likely to result in the serious impairment of the child's health or development. Neglect may occur during pregnancy as a result of maternal substance misuse. Once a child is born, neglect may involve a parent or carer failing to:

○ *provide adequate food, clothing and shelter;*

○ *protect a child from physical and emotional harm or danger;*

○ *ensure adequate supervision;*

○ *ensure access to appropriate medical care or treatment.*

Some possible signs of neglect might include a huge appetite, and dirty and smelly clothes.

Question

What would make you think a child had been injured deliberately?

Answer

○ what is said, what is not said and how it is said;

○ where the injury is on the body, what sort of injury it is and what it looks like;

○ what the child and/or the parent say about the injury;

○ the behaviour of the child/parent – whether the child behaves like a child with an accidental injury, and your experience will help you recognise this.

HISTORICAL PERSPECTIVE

Child protection and safeguarding is not new. Early formal attempts at protecting children date back to 1889 when an Act of Parliament was passed, making cruelty to children illegal. However, at this time, children's welfare was still poorly attended to on a national level and it was down to individuals to do what they could. Of significance in the promotion of children's welfare and their rights were such people as Thomas Coram, Thomas Barnado and Benjamin Waugh, and their legacy is still evident today in their charitable organisations, which live on; namely Coram, Barnado's and the National Society for the Prevention of Cruelty to Children (NSPCC).

Children's rights

In more recent times there have been a number of key cases that have highlighted the need for change and in particular the need for a more cohesive, multi-agency approach. The death of Maria Cowell in 1973, killed by her stepfather, highlighted the lack of co-operation between services (Batty, 2005). This sad case, although not unique, finally led to the Children Act 1989, which aimed to ensure children were protected from abuse and exploitation, with additional rights to inquiries regarding the safeguarding of their welfare.

The Children Act 1989 sets out in detail what local authorities and the courts should do to protect the welfare of children.

It charges local authorities with a duty to:

○ provide '*services for children in need, their families and others*' (section 17);

○ investigate '*if they have reasonable cause to suspect that a child who lives, or is found, in their area is suffering, or is likely to suffer, significant harm*' (section 47).

In 1989, world leaders realised that under-18s needed their own convention because they required additional care and protection that adults did not. This convention, known as The United Nations Convention on the Rights of the Child (UNCRC 1989), was the first legally binding international agreement to incorporate the full range of human rights, including civil, cultural, economic, political and social. The national governments who agreed to undertake these obligations committed to protecting children and upholding their rights, and were willing to be held accountable for these before the international community. The Convention particularly identified that children had the right to protection from abuse, to express their views and have them listened to, and for care and services if they are disabled or living away from home. It is worth noting that although the UK ratified this in 1991, it is not part of UK law.

SIGNIFICANT CASES AND THEIR IMPLICATIONS

✏ Case study

Victoria Climbié

Victoria Climbié came to England from the Ivory Coast in 1999 to live with her aunt. She died in 2000 aged eight as a result of the abuse suffered at the hands of not only her aunt but also her aunt's boyfriend. When she died she had 126 injuries. During the time she was being abused, the police, doctors and social workers had all made contact with her but failed to either diagnose or investigate concerns thoroughly (Littlemore, 2003). Following her death, the government asked Lord Laming to conduct an inquiry (Laming, 2003) to help decide whether new legislation and guidance was needed to improve the child protection system in England.

The government responded with the *Keeping Children Safe* report (DfES, DH and Home Office, 2003) and the *Every Child Matters* (ECM) green paper (DfES, 2003). The green paper proposed a national framework of change for children, focusing on five outcomes:

1. being healthy;

2. staying safe;

3. enjoying and achieving;

4. making a positive contribution;

5. achieving economic well-being.

These recommendations fed into the Children Act 2004. In the following years there was a great focus in education and related services around these five themes and ECM even had its own website. The coalition government of 2010 ceased to support the initiative and it now has a limited profile.

The Children Act 2004

This made it statutory to safeguard and promote the welfare of children across all statutory agencies except education (where it was already statutory in the Education Act 2002). The Act did not replace or even amend much of the Children Act 1989, but its aim was to give extra clarification. It covers England and Wales in different sections. The Act:

o   created the post of Children's Commissioner for England and required local
     authorities to appoint a director of Children's Services and an elected lead member

for Children's Services, who would be held accountable for the delivery of services. Revised guidance on these roles was published in April 2012 (DfE, 2012a);

○ required local authorities and their partners (for example, the police and health service) to work together more cohesively to promote the well-being, safeguarding and welfare of children;

○ created Local Safeguarding Children Boards (LSCB), which also had the role of investigating child deaths in their areas. These are made up of representatives from local partner agencies such as housing, health, police and probation services. The LSCBs co-ordinate the functions of all partner agencies in relation to safeguarding children, which includes co-ordinating and allocating funding and commissioning independent serious case reviews (more on these later);

○ updated the legislation on physical punishment by parents and ensured the defence of it being reasonable physical punishment could not be used if an injury sustained was such that it would be serious enough to warrant a charge of assault.

Case study

The Soham murders

In 2002 two ten-year-old school girls, Holly Wells and Jessica Chapman, were murdered by the caretaker from the local secondary school, Ian Huntley, who was the partner of a teaching assistant from their primary school. During the investigation, it transpired that Huntley had been known to the police in another geographical area for a range of alleged offences, including those of a sexual nature and burglary. However, it appeared that due to a combination of poor record keeping and a lack of co-operation between forces, this information was not shared. Although the police force in which his school was situated had undertaken some form of vetting procedure, this had lacked depth and hence did not identify information that should have come to light.

CRB checks

The subsequent inquiry by Bichard (2005) examined vetting procedures as well as record keeping and information sharing in the police and led to The Safeguarding Vulnerable Groups Act 2006. It established a new centralised vetting and barring scheme for people working with children and also recommended a registration scheme for people working with children and vulnerable adults such as the elderly. The development of this recommendation led to the foundation of the Independent Safeguarding Authority (ISA) and tightening of the Criminal Records Bureau (CRB) checks. The CRB check, originated in March 2002, was against records held on the Police National Computer and also against the list of people barred from working with children, the 'ISA Children's Barred List' (previously known as DfES list 99), which originated in May 2002. Eason (2006) reports that the government suggested that following the Soham murders employers should obtain a CRB Enhanced Disclosure before teachers were placed in a school. Huntley had been employed prior to the CRB checks although, as already indicated, some checks, including a list 99 check, were carried out for his role. The CRB and ISA merged in 2012 and are now known as the Disclosure and Barring Service (DBS), which is responsible for the checks needed on staff who will be working with children or other vulnerable groups. There are two checks, one DBS check and one against the Children's Barred List. Since 2013 it has been possible for employers to check online whether there has been any new information since the original check was issued.

Question

Who would you describe as vulnerable?

Answer

The particularly vulnerable tend to be children with disabilities or special educational needs (SEN), the very young, children of asylum seekers, children of teenage parents, looked-after children and children in poverty. Educators need to be particularly alert to these groups.

 **Case study**

Peter Connelly

Peter Connelly, originally known only as Baby P, was two years old when he died at the hands of his mother, her boyfriend and a lodger in 2007. The case and subsequent serious case review (SCR) identified a series of errors by a range of services that had failed to safeguard the child, and concluded that his death was totally preventable. The SCR noted the importance of training for professionals involved in safeguarding and stated that the LSCB should ensure that the procedures in place were suitably robust. In addition, it stressed the need for the LSCB to work where needed on early intervention.

The subsequent inquiry into child protection was again led by Laming (2009). He noted that too many local authorities had failed to adopt reforms identified in previous reviews, such as his own after the Victoria Climbié case. He recommended that the recruitment, training and supervision of social workers needed to be reviewed. The guidance in

Working Together to Safeguard Children was strengthened, updated and reissued in 2010. In addition, Office for Standards in Education (Ofsted) inspections of local authority Children's Services were to focus more on practice.

These big and shocking cases naturally reach national attention and demonstrate that when things go wrong there will be an inquiry leading to changes in the law and procedures. Inquiries can also be called for when malpractice is discovered in relation to children or there are differences of opinion among professionals. Hence improvements in child protection are continually being attempted.

Developments in multi-agency working

Over recent years the focus has been firmly on multi-agency working. Ultimately, if agencies are working together to ensure child welfare is promoted and safeguarding is effective, the requirement to take steps to protect children from harm is reduced (DCSF, 2009). In 2015 a database will be launched that will help enable National Health Service (NHS) staff to identify children suffering from neglect or abuse as it will show children already subject to a plan or who are regular attenders at hospital (Malik, 2012).

Question

Who do you think might be involved in child protection issues?

Answer

A wide range of organisations such as local authority heads of service, doctors, lawyers, youth engagement experts, probation officers, teachers, police, housing, social services and child health experts. They come together as part of the LSCBs.

Legislation

The key documents that have helped develop multi-agency work are summarised in Table 4.1.

Table 4.1 Safeguarding and child protection legislation

Date	Document	Key themes
1989	Children Act	Collaboration and co-ordination of Children's Services
1999	*Working Together to Safeguard Children: A Guide to Inter-Agency Working to Safeguard and Promote the Welfare of Children*	Set out guidance for working with other agencies
2002	Joint Chief Inspectors' *Safeguarding Children*	Moved towards an all-encompassing approach
2003	Laming Inquiry: *The Victoria Climbié inquiry*	Highlighted failures in multi-agency working

Date	Document	Key themes
2003	Every Child Matters	Aimed to improve outcomes for children
2004	Children Act	Introduced Local Safeguarding Children Boards and Serious Case Reviews
2006	*Working Together to Safeguard Children: A Guide to Inter-Agency Working to Safeguard and Promote the Welfare of Children*	Further updated guidelines that identified the ways in which organisations and individuals should work together to safeguard and promote the well-being of children
2009	Laming Inquiry: *The Protection of Children in England*	Professionals should know children as individuals
2010	*Working Together to Safeguard Children: A Guide to Inter-Agency Working to Safeguard and Promote the Welfare of Children*	Updated guidance following Laming's 2009 report, taking account of recommendations Stressed shared responsibility
2011	*Munro Review of Child Protection: Final Report – a Child-Centred System*	Putting the child at the centre Encouraging the valuing of professional expertise Encouraging the need for early help
2013	*Working Together to Safeguard Children: A Guide to Inter-Agency Working to Safeguard and Promote the Welfare of Children*	Updated guidance emphasising the need for early help
2014	*Keeping Children Safe in Education*	Statutory guidance requiring schools to update polices, including ensuring there is a staff behaviour policy, and understand their individual and collective responsibility. The person responsible in a school for safeguarding is now called the 'designated safeguarding lead'

Question

What do you think are the issues with multi-agency work?

Answer

Potential issues might be as follows.

- Agencies have different professional cultures and knowledge that influence their ethos, aims, priorities, timescales and ways of working (Wilson and James, 2007).

- Practitioners can see multi-disciplinary work as threatening their professional status, creating extra demands on limited time and resources (Anning, 2005).

- There is a lack of understanding of each other's roles (Atkinson et al, 2002).

- Since the cuts in 2010, many of the services that could be involved in child protection have been heavily cut, leading to staff being under increased pressure (Murray, 2013).

INTERVENTION AND PREVENTION

In relation to intervention and prevention, as a TA it is vital to realise that you are working as part of a team and it is suggested that you discuss any concerns or issues with your classteacher or designated safeguarding lead person in the first instance, but remember that anybody can make a referral to children's social care. By being aware of the indicators of child abuse, you will be in a position to help intervene and prevent situations escalating. Families can be connected to the services they need and get the help required to reduce risks. There are many factors that increase a child's chances of being at risk and the DfE (2013) highlight this in the current *Working Together to Safeguard Children* (DfE, 2013) document, which particularly emphasises that early help is of vital importance for a child who is:

- disabled or has specific additional needs or special educational needs;

- a young carer;

- showing signs of engaging in criminal behaviour;

- in a family circumstance presenting challenges for the child, such as substance misuse, adult mental health, domestic violence;

- showing early signs of abuse and/or neglect.

(DfE, 2013, p 12)

Children growing up in poverty are also identified as being at risk.

The Common Assessment Framework

It is for the children in these families where co-ordinated support from more than one agency would be of assistance. Such early help assessments may involve the use of the Common Assessment Framework (CAF) and should assist in identifying where families require help, preventing their situation from escalating to the need for intervention under the Children Act 1989. Information sharing is essential for effective identification, assessment and provision, and guidance is offered on what can be shared and the circumstances in which this can happen (DCSF, 2008).

The CAF system was recommended as part of the ECM green paper (DCSF, 2003) and was eventually implemented in 2006. The CAF was intended to bring cohesion to a system where agencies often had their own assessment processes and there was a need to have a more co-ordinated approach. It is a shared assessment and planning framework for use across all Children's Services and all local areas in England. Undertaken at the first signs of difficulty, it aims to help the early identification of children's additional needs and promote co-ordinated service provision to meet them. The CAF is a standardised approach to conducting an assessment of a child's additional needs and deciding how those needs should be met (Kendall, Rodger and Palmer, 2009). It offers a framework that helps professionals working with children and their families to assess their needs and aim for earlier effective services and the development of a shared understanding between services of those needs. There are four levels of support, shown in Table 4.2.

Table 4.2 The four levels of support

Level 1: Universal
This includes children whose needs are being met by universal services, such as housing, mainstream education, primary health care, community resources and children's centres, with telephone advice and occasional visits. Children here are thriving.
Level 2: Vulnerable children and young people
Children in this category are likely to require a CAF to be undertaken, which may possibly identify the need for some short-term interventions from services. At this stage, Children's Social Care is not essential but the identification of early stresses and provision of services may reduce the likelihood of escalating problems. Children here are described as just coping and have emerging or are presenting with additional needs and are likely to be in need of some early help.
Level 3: Children in need
This refers to children who have a high risk of their health and development being impaired without assessment and intervention and where there are more complex difficulties. Such children may be likely to move into level 4 without the provision of services based on assessed needs. These may also include children who have been assessed at level 4 in the recent past. A CAF should definitely have been instigated.
Level 4: Significant harm
These children and young people are at risk of/suffering from significant harm and it is difficult to achieve change to reduce risk. They might include:
o children about whom there is a serious concern related to their care, health or development, and/or the child has or is likely to suffer significant harm without intervention;
o a child who is experiencing serious family dysfunction, a child who is beyond control where no person has exercised or is able to exercise parental responsibility or the child is abandoned or neglected.

The LSCB offers guidance on what a CAF should consist of and the relevant paperwork for that authority, as well as information on who to approach for advice. Once the CAF process is implemented, an assessment can take place and the lead professional and the team around the child (TAC) can be implemented in order to provide the required services (DfE 2012b).

Having a CAF in place may reduce the chances of harm, but note that a CAF is not for children who you think are suffering from some kind of abuse.

Case studies

1. Kerry is ten years old and lives with her mum and step-dad of five years. Both adults allegedly smoke cannabis and recently they have not been getting on well, resulting in verbal and sometime physical abuse, although this is rarely in front of Kerry. Recently Kerry was picked up from school by her mum, who appeared unsteady on her feet.

2. A family of four children attend the school. They are unkempt and small for their age. They are on free school meals and are always very hungry at lunch time. The parents rarely come to parents' evening and there are rumours that Mum is an alcoholic. Dad often works away.

3. Dan is 11 years old. He is a happy child, although from what appears to be quite a deprived background. The family has previously been known to social services but was never particularly co-operative and there appears to be no current involvement. Recently, Dan has become withdrawn and sullen.

4. Sandra is a single parent who is working part-time as a solicitor near to where the family lives. On the mornings she needs to work, she leaves early so her three children, aged 11, 9 and 7, are at home for an hour before they walk to school, which is at the end of the road.

Question

Consider the case studies above, imagining you work at the school the children attend. Based on what you know, would you talk to the designated safeguarding lead about instigating a CAF or making a referral to social services? Do you think there is any abuse taking place? What action might you take in each of these examples?

Answer

If you suggested either a CAF or even a referral to social services for all scenarios you would not be wrong. In all cases, it is likely to have come to the attention of school and a conversation with parents by the head may also be a starting point, unless it is felt that the children are actually in immediate danger. You may also have suggested emotional abuse or neglect for question 1; and if you suggested neglect for questions 2, 3 and 4 you would be right.

Framework for the assessment of need

More detailed assessments can also be made and it is vital that as much information as possible is gathered. It is helpful to consider the factors, and their interactions, outlined in the assessment triangle in Figure 4.1.

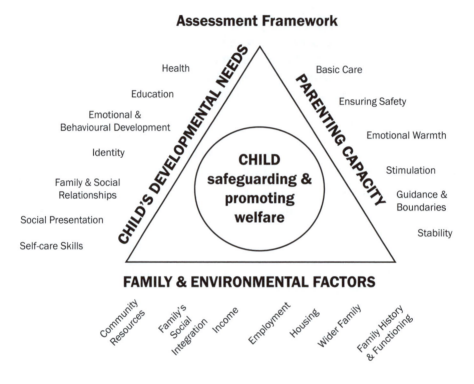

Figure 4.1 The Assessment Framework diagram. Taken from *Working Together to Safeguard Children* (DfE, 2013), p 20. Crown Copyright

The Framework helps provide a way of analysing, understanding and recording what is happening to the child and their family. The CAF and the assessment triangle have a great deal in common; indeed, the CAF was designed with the assessment triangle in mind. The CAF is an earlier assessment and may indicate that a more detailed assessment is needed.

Roles and responsibilities in relation to child protection

Under the Children Act 2004, everyone who works with families and children has a responsibility to help safeguard children. In particular, school governors and heads must ensure that there are polices in place which are reviewed annually, that there is safe recruitment, appropriate staff training and that there is a designated safeguarding lead. In addition, schools should operate safeguarding in relation to bullying and equal opportunities.

Policies and procedures

Educational establishments are required to have policies and procedures in place in relation to child protection and safeguarding.

Policy checklist

Activity

○   It is a good idea to reflect on your organisation's policies. Obtain a copy of the child protection/safeguarding policy for your setting and assess its effectiveness using the following policy checklist.

–   How do staff or volunteers obtain access to the procedures?

–   What should staff do if there is an immediate threat of abuse to a child?

–   Can a child be medically examined without their parent's consent?

–   What would you do if you had a child protection concern about a child?

–   What should staff members do regarding promises of confidentiality to children?

–   What action should be taken if a staff member or volunteer sees one child abusing another?

–   What action should be taken by a staff member or volunteer who suspects another member of staff of abusing a child? Who would they ask for advice?

–   Who conducts an enquiry into a report of child abuse within the setting?

–   What should a member of staff do if a senior manager advises them not to refer a child protection concern to children's social care but to allow the matter to be dealt with internally?

–   How often do the child protection procedures have to be reviewed?

Taking action

You need to be observant and vigilant in relation to child protection and safeguarding, and you need to know what to do if you suspect abuse or neglect. There is a requirement for people working with children to keep children safe (DfE, 2013). However, you will not be subject to criminal proceedings if you fail to report concerns, although you could be subject to professional disciplinary reviews (NSPCC, 2013). Discussion and sharing is important as you may actually hold the final piece of the jigsaw in multi-agency work. The first step is to talk to your designated safeguarding lead.

Child-initiated concerns

Sometimes you may suspect nothing until a child discloses something to you. Lindon (2012) notes that children may tell you directly or they may tell you through their actions.

Remember the importance of listening attentively and being supportive (NSPCC, 2010), but be guided by the situation in which the child is disclosing. They may have deliberately told you when you are partially distracted by something else as this makes it easier to talk to you about it. Do not ask leading questions but ascertain the facts by asking when, where, who and what. If a child does disclose, it is important to empathise but avoid criticising as the abuser is often a relative who is still loved.

It is also important that you don't agree to keeping it a secret and that you avoid asking too many questions that may subsequently jeopardise a criminal investigation. The key thing is to remember the five Rs: receive, reassure, respond, record and refer.

Even if you have some doubts, share the information with the appropriate person in your setting. There are also other organisations where you can go for advice, such as the police, social services, the NHS, the NSPCC and the LSCB.

What to do if you suspect a colleague

If this situation arises, raise the concern with the designated safeguarding lead. If a child tells you directly, you must gain sufficient facts and then discuss this with the designated safeguarding lead, and ultimately the case will be referred to the LSCB for further investigation by the Local Authority Designated Officer (LADO). The LADO works within Children's Services and should be alerted to all cases of this kind of allegation.

Following a concern under section 47 of the Children Act 2004, after initial investigation, and if appropriate, a child protection conference should be held within 15 working days.

Child protection conferences:

o come after social services make an assessment based on the 'assessment framework triangle';

o have a report submitted (parents receive a copy);

o are multi-agency;

o are run on behalf of LSCB;

o have an independent chair;

o may have the alleged perpetrator present with their legal advisors;

o may exclude people from certain parts;

o may result in a child protection plan;

o should lead to a core group to support the child and family.

Following the child protection conference there will be follow-up meetings and regular reviews, all within dictated timescales.

It is worth noting that things can still go wrong even if children are subject to a child protection plan. Peter Connelly was under one when he died.

CONCLUSION

Children have the right to grow up in safety and free from harm, and you play an important role in helping the children you work with to do that. Remember that you do not work in isolation and there are plenty of people with whom you can share your concerns.

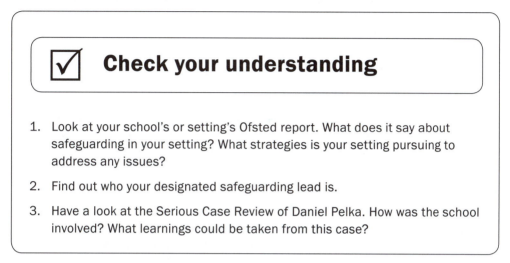

☑ **Check your understanding**

1. Look at your school's or setting's Ofsted report. What does it say about safeguarding in your setting? What strategies is your setting pursuing to address any issues?

2. Find out who your designated safeguarding lead is.

3. Have a look at the Serious Case Review of Daniel Pelka. How was the school involved? What learnings could be taken from this case?

▶▶ **TAKING IT FURTHER**

DfE (2013) *Working Together to Safeguard Children: A Guide to Inter-Agency Working to Safeguard and Promote the Welfare of Children*. London: DfE.

DfE (2014) *Preventing and Tackling Bullying. Advice for Headteachers, Staff and Governors*. London: DfE.

DH (2002) *Safeguarding Children: A Joint Chief Inspectors' Report on Arrangements to Safeguard Children*. London: DH Publications.

A range of useful documents at: www.safeguardinginschools.co.uk/andrew-hall/

REFERENCES

Anning, A (2005) Investigating the Impact of Working in Multi-Agency Service Delivery Settings in the UK on Early Years Practitioners' Beliefs and Practices. *Journal of Early Childhood Research* 3(19): 19–50.

Atkinson, M, Wilkin, A, Stott, A, Doherty, P and Kinder, K (2002) *Multi-Agency Working: A Detailed Case Study*. London: National Foundation for Educational Research.

Batty, D (2005) Timeline: A History of Child Protection. *The Guardian*: 18 July.

Bichard, M (2005) *The Bichard Inquiry Report*. London: Cabinet Office.

DCSF (2003) *Working Together to Safeguard Children: A Guide to Inter-Agency Working to Safeguard and Promote the Welfare of Children*. Nottingham: DCSF.

DCSF (2008) *Information Sharing: Guidance for Practitioners and Managers*. Nottingham: DCSF.

DCSF (2009) *Working Together to Safeguard Children Consultation Document: A Guide to Inter-Agency Working to Safeguard and Promote the Welfare of Children*. Nottingham: DCSF.

DfE (2013) *Working Together to Safeguard Children: A Guide to Inter-Agency Working to Safeguard and Promote the Welfare of Children*. London: DfE.

DfES (2003) *Every Child Matters*. Norwich: TSO.

DfES, DH and Home Office (2003) *Keeping Children Safe: The Government's Response to the Victoria Climbié Inquiry Report and Joint Chief Inspectors' Report Safeguarding Children*. Norwich: TSO.

Department for Education (DfE) (2012a) *Statutory Guidance on the Roles and Responsibilities of the Director of Children's Services and the Lead Member for Children's Services*. London: DfE.

DfE (2012b) Team around the Child (TAC). [online] Available at: http://webarchive. nationalarchives.gov.uk/20130903161404/http://www.education.gov.uk/ childrenandyoungpeople/strategy/integratedworking/a0068944/team-around-the-child-tac.

Eason, G (2006) *Concerns About Teachers' List 99*. BBC News, 14 January.

Great Britain: The Children Act (1989) London: TSO.

Great Britain: The Children Act (2004) London: TSO.

Great Britain: The Education Act (2002) London: TSO.

Great Britain: The Safeguarding Vulnerable Groups Act (2006) London: TSO.

Kendall, S, Rodger, J and Palmer, H (2009) *The Use of Whole Family Assessment to Identify the Needs of Families with Multiple Problems*. London: DfE.

Laming, H (2003) *The Victoria Climbié Inquiry: Report of an Inquiry by Lord Laming*. Norwich: TSO.

Laming, H (2009) *The Protection of Children in England: A Progress Report*. Norwich TSO.

Lindon, J (2012) *Safeguarding and Child Protection: 0–8 Years* (4th edn). Abingdon: Hodder Education.

Littlemore, S (2003) Victoria Climbié: Chain of Neglect. BBC News, 28 January.

Malik, S (2012) Every Child Visiting A&E to be Logged in National Database from 2015. *The Guardian*, 27 December 2012.

Munro, E (2011) *Munro Review of Child Protection: Final Report – a Child-Centred System*. Norwich TSO.

Murray, K (2013) Social Care: Under Pressure Like Never Before. *The Guardian*, 16 October.

NSPCC (2010) *Listening to Safeguard a Child (1)*. London: NSPCC.

NSPCC (2013) *Child Abuse Reporting Requirements for Professionals: NSPCC Factsheet.* November 2013.

Training and Development Agency for Schools (TDA) (2007) Higher Level Teaching Assistant Candidate Handbook. London: TDA. [online] Available at: www.education.gov.uk/ publications/eOrderingDownload/TDA0420.pdf (accessed August 2014).

UNCRC (1989) *United Nations Convention on the Rights of the Child*. UNICEF.

Wilson, K and James, A (2007) *The Child Protection Handbook* (3rd edn). London: Elsevier.

5 Inclusion and special educational needs

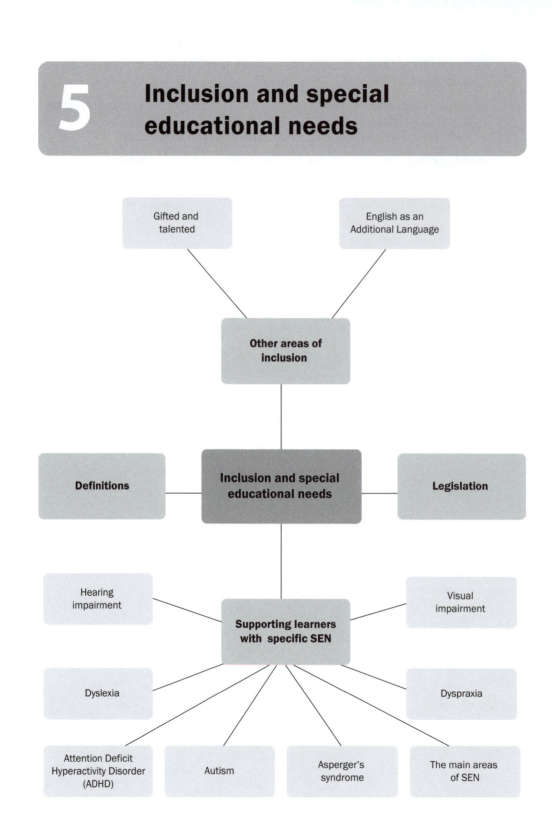

INTRODUCTION

This chapter examines the area of inclusion and special educational needs and disability (SEND). It will include the historical context that has led to current practices and the recent changes to legislation. It outlines how to recognise SEN and identifies support strategies to aid inclusion.

STARTING POINT

What do you understand by the terms inclusion and SEN?

Spend some time reflecting on these concepts.

- ○ What do they mean to you?
- ○ How do they apply to your setting?

DEFINITIONS

Inclusion

In the 2013 revised national curriculum (Department for Education (DfE), 2013) the inclusion statement has two principles:

- ○ *'setting suitable challenges;*
- ○ *responding to pupils' needs and overcoming potential barriers for individuals and groups of pupils'.*

(DfE, 2013, p 9)

The new curriculum emphasises stretching work and ambitious targets.

Crossley suggests inclusion could be *'referred to as "integration", in the sense that children who might previously have been educated in a special educational setting should instead have the opportunity to receive their education in a mainstream school wherever possible'* (2013, p 141). However, Nutbrown and Clough explain that *'Inclusion may be seen as the drive towards maximal participation in and minimal exclusion from early years settings, from school and from society'* (2006, p 3).

As you can see, there are different interpretations, so it is important to make sure you understand what your setting means by this term and check the policy.

Special educational needs

The DfE (2014) has defined children with SEN in the following way:

> *A child or young person has SEN if they have a learning difficulty or disability which calls for special educational provision to be made for them. A child of compulsory school age or a young person has a learning difficulty or disability if they:*
>
> (a) *have a significantly greater difficulty in learning than the majority of others of the same age; or*
> (b) *have a disability which prevents or hinders them from making use of educational facilities of a kind generally provided for others of the same age in mainstream schools or mainstream post-16 institutions.*
>
> *A child under compulsory school age has special educational needs if they fall within the definition at (a) or (b) above or would so do if special educational provision was not made for them.*
>
> *This is a broad definition covering children and young people from 0–25 years of age.*

(Special Educational Needs and Disability (SEND)
Code of Practice, DfE, 2014, Foreword)

Again, it is important to check your own policies, but what is clear is that there is an expectation for children with SEN to make appropriate progress and to have work that is appropriate for them, suitable for their needs and provides the appropriate challenge for them. Children are usually educated in mainstream settings and the environment can be adapted to ensure inclusion. Have a look at the case study regarding inclusion.

 **Case study**

Ansar

Ansar is a lively and caring 11-year-old boy. He was born with moderate learning difficulties due to complications with his birth and is currently working below the expectations for his age. English is not his first language and as a result he struggles with English in school. He has gross motor difficulties and can find working with others a challenge, and he finds socialising with other children his age quite difficult. The gap between his development and capabilities compared with those of his peers has widened over the years. When he was in Year 4 it was decided that he should remain there as it was felt it was easier to include him with some of the activities that the rest of the class were doing. Even in Year 4, due to Ansar's developmental delays, all his work is differentiated and an increasing amount is unrelated to that of his peers. He has built up a strong relationship with the teacher and TA in the class. However, although he responds well to the staff, Ansar is removed from the class with increasing frequency as he can be disruptive. The TA regularly gives Ansar personal support and Ansar enjoys playing with the other children in his class. However, the school feels that Ansar will not cope in a large mainstream secondary school and has suggested he goes to a secondary school for pupils with moderate learning difficulties.

Question

Who do you think would be involved in this decision?

Answer

It is a lengthy process involving a range of professionals including the local authority, the school (headteachers, teachers, Special Educational Needs Co-ordinators (SENCOs), social workers, specialist support staff (such as educational psychologists, speech and language therapists) and parents. It is lengthy because it is important to make the right decision that best caters for the needs of the child and it is important that people who understand the child's needs and difficulties be involved (adapted from Crossley, 2013).

LEGISLATION

The area of inclusion and SEN is constantly shifting and there has been a wealth of relevant legislation over the years. Table 5.1 indicates some of the main legislation and its implications for children with SEN.

Table 5.1 SEND and inclusion legislation

Date	Document	Key themes
1978	The Warnock Report	o Recommendations regarding children with SEN in relation to their medical needs, school and employment o Change in terminology o Responsibility for heads to monitor progress o Designated teacher for SEN o Appropriate curricular provision o Fed into the 1981 Education Act
1981	Education Act	o Obligation by local authorities to provide assessment for SEN o Inclusion of children with SEN in mainstream settings o Statements of SEN
1993	Education Act	o Requirement for Code of Practice relating to SEN to provide guidelines to local authorities and governing bodies
1994	Special Educational Needs Code of Practice	o Individual Education Plan (IEP) – focused support through a staged approach o Statements of special educational need o Requirement to appoint SENCO
1996	Education Act	o Consolidated the 1993 Act
2001	Special Educational Needs and Disability Act (SENDA)	o Consolidated commitment to educate children with SEN in mainstream schools o Increased parental rights to appeal o Also led to amendment of 1996 Education Act, which stated children with SEN must be educated in mainstream setting unless it would prove ineffective and against parental wishes
2001	Special Educational Needs Code of Practice	o Incorporated changes instigated in SENDA o IEPs altered and more action-orientated, called 'school action' and 'school action plus' o Classteachers to take greater responsibility
2010	The Equality Act	o Learners and staff need to be protected from discrimination, victimisation and harassment o Employers are required to make reasonable adjustments to working environments o Brought all anti-discrimination legislation under one umbrella
2014	Children and Families Act	o A single assessment process o Statements of SEN to be replaced by Education Health and Care Plan (EHCP) o Optional budgets for parents to buy support

Table 5.1 (cont.)

Date	Document	Key themes
2014	Special Educational Needs and Disability Code of Practice	○ Covers 0–5 years ○ Encourages teachers to identify and assess the needs of all children ○ Emphasises the importance of getting the right interventions ○ Ensures better monitoring and evaluation ○ Expects whole-school collaboration regarding SEN ○ Close working between SENCO, teachers and TAs ○ Expects children and families to have greater involvement ○ Identifies the need for early intervention ○ Identifies a 'graduated approach' of action: assess, plan, do, review ○ Removes 'school action' and 'school action plus'

SUPPORTING LEARNERS WITH SPECIFIC SEN

Working in schools, you will come across a diverse group of learners, some of whom will need additional support because of their SEN. TAs are often called upon to provide this support, and if you are it may be possible to attend additional training to help you do this to the best of your ability. However, your teacher and SENCO should also be able to offer you advice, and, of course, if you are going to spend a reasonable amount of time with an individual then you will no doubt research how best to do this yourself. There has, however, been growing concern regarding the support provided for children with SEN. It has been shown that pupils with SEN may spend over a quarter of their week away from their class and teacher, and this separation impacts not only on their education but also on their social development. Children often work with TAs who are ill equipped to do this job (Webster and Blatchford, 2013) so it is vital that you take any opportunity that you can to find out how best to work with the children in your class.

The main areas of SEN

The range of SEN is enormous and it is important to realise that every child is an individual and will behave and respond differently from someone else with the same or similar diagnosis of need.

Under the 2014 SEND Code of Practice there are four main areas of need within which SEND falls.

1. Communication and interaction

   Within this category you will come across children with:

   ○ autism-spectrum conditions, including Asperger's;

- speech and language difficulties;

- English as an Additional Language (EAL) (though not in itself a SEN);

- Attention Deficit Hyperactivity Disorder (ADHD).

2. Cognition and learning

- dyslexia;

- moderate learning difficulties;

- speech and language difficulties;

- dyspraxia;

- ADHD.

3. Social, mental and emotional health

- attachment disorder;

- ADHD;

- autism;

- Tourette's syndrome;

- mental health problems.

4. Sensory and/or physical

- wheelchair users;

- hearing impairment;

- visual impairment;

- degenerative illness, eg muscular dystrophy;

- dyspraxia.

Some SEN leads to behavioural difficulties and often the usual behaviour-management techniques will work, but the child will often have a specific personalised plan with clear targets to achieve, which may relate to their behaviour as well as learning. For a TA, one key support mechanism can be helping children understand why they behave the way they do. Showing that you care can often help them to open up about their behaviour.

In this section some of the more common SEN that you may come across in mainstream schools will be discussed alongside some of the strategies. This is not an exhaustive list and there are specialist websites that can give you more details.

Autism

What is it?

Autism is a lifelong development disorder that affects how people think, communicate and make sense of the world around them. This is often described as the triad of impairments, with people have varying difficulty under the three headings of:

- Social communication. In this area, people:

  - have difficulty processing language and interpreting facial expressions, body language or tone of voice;

  - take things literally so have trouble with metaphors and figures of speech;

  - have difficulty with sarcasm;

  - have difficulty following long or complicated sentences;

  - have difficulty explaining how they feel.

- Social interaction. In this area, people:

  - avoid eye contact;

  - are unaware of personal space;

  - are unable to interpret others' emotions;

  - may laugh or speak at inappropriate times;

  - show no interest in others' opinions or interests.

- Social imagination. In this area, people:

  - find it difficult to see another's perspective;

  - find it difficult to interpret others' feelings;

  - fail to understand the concept of danger;

  - find imaginative play difficult;

  - find it difficult to plan for change or the future;

  - find it difficult to cope in a new situation.

(The National Autistic Society, 2014)

The National Autistic Society (2014) describes autism as existing along a spectrum, which means that people with autism share certain areas of difficulty but their condition will affect them in different ways. Some people will be able to live fairly independent lives, while others may need long-term support.

How can learners be supported?

Inclusion of learners with autism has become an important issue within education in recent years, as many children do remain in a mainstream setting. Once teachers and TAs have gained knowledge on the triad of impairments, they can then work out how to support an individual's learning and adapt the learning to their needs. A child with autism requires a regular routine of a visual nature, which helps focus them on where their attention needs to be directed. Many children with autism need an environment free from clutter. Schools may make use of visual aids such as the Pictorial Exchange Communication System (PECS) to help children communicate. PECS involves exchanging pictures for items the child wants, and it can eventually build up to enable more advanced communication. Another technique that is used is called Relationship

Development Intervention® (RDI). This is a behavioural treatment that helps children to develop flexibility. It aims to help individuals with autism form personal relationships by gradually strengthening the building blocks of social connections. This includes the ability to form an emotional bond and share experiences. Children with autism also benefit from visual timetables.

Asperger's syndrome

What is it?

Asperger's syndrome is a developmental disorder resembling autism, characterised by impaired social interaction, repetitive patterns of behaviour and restricted interests. People with Asperger's syndrome usually have normal language and cognitive development and often have average or above average intelligence. They may also have difficulty in the same three areas already mentioned, but Asperger's is often referred to as higher functioning autism. Some children will struggle with over- or under-sensitivity to sounds, touch, taste, light, smells and colours, and this sometimes also applies to children with autism (The National Autistic Society, 2014).

In the classroom, children with Asperger's syndrome may exhibit certain characteristics such as:

o   lack of focus;

o   abnormal eye contact;

o   literal thinking;

o   difficulty with fine-motor skills;

o   lack of understanding of social cues and personal space;

o   tendency to speak bluntly without regard for impact of words on others;

o   poor organisational skills;

o   difficulty with learning in large groups.

(Hutton, 2014)

How can learners be supported?

Some children may benefit from one-to-one support or specific interventions in relation to social and communication development. Some examples are given here.

o   Be aware of speaking literally – try not to use sarcasm or idioms and translate these when needed.

o   Be aware of any particular triggers – loud sounds, unfamiliar textures, over-stimulation.

o   Differentiate work to challenge the child in areas that interest them.

o   Develop routines and try to keep to them, and warn children clearly and in detail if things need to change.

○ Implement changes gradually where possible.

○ Be aware of the issues group work may cause and be prepared to mediate.

Visual impairment

What is it?

Visual impairment is an umbrella term for a wide variety of conditions and includes a range of difficulties from short-sightedness to blindness. Visual impairment is when a person has sight loss that cannot be fully corrected using glasses or contact lenses. Children with visual impairment often have complex needs, for example, using Braille imposes additional cognitive demands. Severe examples of visual impairment include tunnel vision, squints, myopia or profound degrees of low vision. Visual impairments are usually identified relatively early in a child's life as babies are monitored and children's vison will be checked as a matter of course at the two-year-old health check and again when they start school (National Health Service (NHS), 2014a). Early identification ensures that systems are in place to correctly support the child at school. Children with visual impairment can suffer as a result of teachers having different expectations regarding achievement, although there is no obvious correlation between visual impairment and intelligence. However, there will be additional barriers such as the speed at which a child can work, communication skills (relating to reading or writing), spatial awareness and social interaction as there is a reduced capacity to recognise body language and facial expressions.

How can learners be supported?

○ Ensure that children take part in group work that promotes their cognitive, linguistic and social development.

○ Allow children opportunities to rest their eyes.

○ Develop strong liaison between specialists and classroom staff.

○ Use enlarged text and consider the colour of the background and print.

○ Think about positioning in the classroom.

○ Keep classrooms orderly and walkways clear.

○ Use textured labels and strips around the room.

○ Make use of specialist equipment such as magnifiers and electronic text readers.

○ Avoid glare.

Hearing impairment

What is it?

Hearing impairment can be defined as the temporary or permanent loss of some or all hearing in one or both ears. Children with hearing complications have a range of difficulties, from frequent ear infections, perforated ear drums and tinnitus to complete hearing loss. Deafness is classified as mild, moderate, moderately severe, severe and profound. Any issues regarding a child's hearing should become apparent as babies but the two-year-old health check will also assess a child's hearing. One issue is that a hearing impairment may be mistaken for language difficulties (NHS, 2014b).

How can learners be supported?

○ Have a well-lit classroom so children will be able to lip-read more easily.

○ Avoid beards and moustaches as these make lip-reading difficult.

○ Speak clearly with eye contact and face children with a hearing impairment.

○ Use specialist equipment such as radio aids.

○ Think about positioning in the classroom.

○ Make use of visual clues.

○ Equip classrooms with speakers and microphones.

○ Use carpets to absorb unwanted noise.

Dyspraxia

What is it?

Dyspraxia is a developmental co-ordination disorder that affects fine and gross motor skills, which may also include speech.

There are two types of dyspraxia: acquired dyspraxia, which may occur as a result of brain damage, and developmental dyspraxia, where a child is born with the condition. Children are often labelled as clumsy, messy, forgetful or daydreamers. Although the exact causes of dyspraxia are not known, it is thought to be caused by a disruption in the way messages from the brain are transmitted to the body, which affects a person's ability to perform smooth co-ordinated movements. Children with dyspraxia may have difficulties with perception, memory, fine and gross motor skills, articulation and speech, co-ordination, behaviour, progress and attainment, and handwriting. All of these can affect their learning. At school, these can manifest themselves in poor handwriting, lack of co-ordination in PE, difficulty learning new skills and being disorganised (Blamires, 2004).

How can learners be supported?

○ Make effective use of praise to aid self-esteem.

○ Allow extra time.

○ Break tasks into manageable steps.

○ Give opportunities for rest.

○ Avoid copying from the board.

○ Check understanding.

○ Provide one-to-one support in class when possible.

- Remove distractions.

- Work with the child to develop strategies such as 'to do' lists.

- Discuss and plan for change.

Attention Deficit Hyperactivity Disorder (ADHD)

What is it?

ADHD is described as a group of behavioural symptoms that include inattentiveness, hyperactivity and impulsiveness. This can be evident in the following ways:

- lack of attention to detail and a tendency to make careless mistakes;

- messy and careless work;

- easily distracted;

- inability to sustain attention on tasks or activities;

- difficulty finishing schoolwork or performing tasks that need concentration;

- lack of focus on one task and frequent movement to another;

- disorganised work habits;

- forgetfulness in daily activities (for example, missing appointments, forgetting to bring lunch);

- failure to complete tasks such as homework;

- lack of concentration during conversations, not listening to others and not following details or rules of activities in social situations.

(NHS, 2014c)

How can learners be supported?

There is no cure for ADHD, but it can be managed through medication, cognitive behavioural therapy and diet. In addition, appropriate advice and support for the individual and parents in partnership with schools can help manage the behaviour (NHS, 2014c). Here are some classroom strategies.

- Model behaviour and encourage good behaviour with healthy praise or rewards.

- Negatively reinforce bad behaviour by allowing appropriate consequences to occur naturally.

- Provide structure and routine.

- Ensure the child has understood instructions by asking them to look at you and repeat them.

- Allow time-out options (such as the toilet).

- Assist the child to make a list of steps needed to get to the goal.

- Use a checklist and chart progress to make it more fun.

- Set up a behaviour contract with support for calming down.

- Prompt helpful self-talk (eg 'I need to think things through before I act').

- Provide stress balls or something similar for long periods of quiet time or sitting still.

Dyslexia

What is it?

According to the British Dyslexia Association (2014) dyslexia occurs on a spectrum, with the symptoms ranging from mild to severe. People with dyslexia find difficulty with:

- phonological awareness (the ability to identify that words are made up of small units of sound called phonemes);

- verbal memory (the ability to remember a short set of instructions);

- rapid serial naming (the ability to quickly name a series of objects or colours);

- verbal processing speed (the time taken to recognise familiar verbal information).

Dyslexia is thought to be relatively common and may be evident in around one in ten people. English can be a particularly challenging language for people with dyslexia because of its inconsistency. Dyslexia is independent of intelligence; the earlier it is identified, the better, as this can avoid the inevitable self-esteem issues that begin to arise when children fall behind their peers. Many people with dyslexia report that the words appear to move around on the page and there is commonly confusion between certain letters such as 'b' and 'd' or 'p' and 'g'. You may also see that the standard of the child's written work does not match their oral ability and their handwriting may be poor with many 'reversals'. Their spelling will be poor and they may produce many variations of the same word, often not phonetically viable. In reading there is likely to be poor comprehension and difficulty with blending phonemes. There may also be evidence in their numeracy work, and time is a particularly difficult concept. Children may also employ work-avoidance tactics, may be easily distracted, take on the role of class clown or be unusually tired with no other explanation (brought about by the concentration required). As the dyslexic brain is believed to process information differently it is advised that a child is supported by someone with specific training in the subject.

How can learners be supported?

Some children benefit from coloured overlays, coloured paper, coloured backgrounds on presentation slides and tinted glasses, although they will need testing to ascertain which colour works best for them. Some fonts are more dyslexic-friendly than others, for example Comic Sans. It is also advised that you check whether they are happy to read aloud in front of others and reduce the amount of copying from a screen. If possible, look for different ways to present work so that children don't always have to write things down. In addition, reduce glare on paper and screens. Finally, provide support with spellings as needed. A range of resources have been developed to help children with dyslexia, including dyslexia-friendly reading schemes such as Alpha to Omega and the Hickey Multisensory Language Course. Toe by Toe is also a useful resource and ReadWrite Inc offers structured practice in decoding words. There are also specific computerised resources such as Nessy, Lexia and Wordshark, some of which link to the dyslexia-friendly reading schemes.

OTHER AREAS OF INCLUSION

Gifted and talented

What is it?

According to Bailey (2004), a child is usually labelled as gifted if they are performing well above the expected level for their age in an academic subject. A talented child is usually one who is exhibiting exceptional levels for their age in a skill usually related to art, sport or music. It is expected that in any class between 5 and 10 per cent of children would fall into this category. If left unidentified, so-called gifted children are likely to underachieve, and if they are not sufficiently challenged they can become disruptive. An obvious flaw in this definition is that a child identified as gifted in one school may not be so identified in another; however, schools should strive to identify such children and provide accordingly, although obviously not at the expense of other children.

How can learners be supported?

There is no one strategy that can be employed to support gifted and talented children and a range of options are available and may be suitable.

- Personalise learning.
- Provide opportunities for learners to progress at their own pace.
- Provide out-of-hours opportunities.
- Encourage participation in local clubs.
- Identify areas and provide opportunities where all children can aim for mastery in a subject.
- Provide opportunities for children to make their own choices in relation to study.
- Identify ways of working in partnership with other schools to develop gifted and talented children.
- Ensure high expectations are set for children.
- Provide structured interventions.
- Assist children in developing higher level thinking.

English as an Additional Language

What is it?

We live in a multilingual country and English is not the home language for many children in schools. Around 16 per cent of primary-aged children speak another language as well as English. There have been a range of governmental strategies over the years to approach this, including the provision of additional funding. The current governmental thinking appears to be focusing on the need for children and their families to speak English (Northcote, 2014). Care must be taken to make sure that children with EAL are not assumed to be of low ability, and the inclusion statement in the 2013 national curriculum identifies that schools should have high expectations of all children (DfE, 2013). Language is tied up with who we are and it is important to recognise and respect children's home language. Some children may well be classed as bilingual, but it is also worth remembering that they may have differing levels of competence in each language. It is vital that home languages are valued as this has been shown to aid academic achievement, no doubt because it also helps with a child's self-esteem (Northcote, 2014).

How can learners be supported?

Remember that children learn language by listening, speaking, reading and then writing, and learning a second language is no different. Children can be supported in the classroom in a range of ways, some more suitable to younger learners and some more appropriate for older learners.

- bilingual staff/interpreter;
- bilingual dictionaries;
- interventions;
- visual timetables;
- visual signs/symbols;
- peer support;
- role play and free play;
- modelling, including the use of standard English;
- opportunities for small-group work where children can use their home language;
- learning some words and phrases of the children's home language;
- celebrating individual culture;
- word banks;
- including other languages and resources in displays, books, etc.

✏️ Case studies

1. Fahrida is six years old, very good at mathematics and really enjoys it. Her parents work with her at home and are finding that she enjoys working with her 12-year-old brother on his mathematics homework. In school, she is becoming bored with what is being presented as she finds it easy.

2. Peter is in Year 4 and excels at football. He plays at lunch time in school and he is noticeably skilful but can be seen to get frustrated with the skills of the other children. You run the school football team, which is usually reserved for the Year 6 boys.

3. Marcel is six years old and recently arrived from Germany. He communicates well in German for his age. He has been to kindergarten. His parents speak a little English and he seems to understand a little English.

4. Anna has been diagnosed with dyslexia and is still struggling to word-build due to gaps in her phonological knowledge. She is in Year 4 and her classteacher is considering sending her to Year 2 every day for their 20-minute phonics lesson. You work closely with Anna so the classteacher asks you what you think.

Questions

○   In case 1, what could the school do to meet Fahrida's needs? How could you as a TA help?

○   In case 2, how could you support Peter?

○   What could you do to help Marcel (case 3) integrate into the classroom?

○   In case 4, what might you say?

Answers

You may have suggested a range of suitable strategies based on your own knowledge and reading, but it is worth noting that moving classes and peer groups is not always the best option. It does not always enhance children's self-concept and needs managing carefully as it does cause disruption, although the targeted activities can be great.

CONCLUSION

Ultimately, inclusion is about differentiation, which must ensure *'the provision of learning opportunities and activities for individuals in particular classrooms'* (Bearne and Kennedy, 2014, p 358), and teachers and TAs should be working together to provide the best opportunities possible.

 Check your understanding

1. Look at your school's or setting's policy on inclusion. Do you feel it is comprehensive and tackles the real issues?

2. Talk to your SENCO. Ask how the school is meeting the challenges of the recent changes to the provision of SEN brought about by the 2014 Children and Families Act and the 2014 SEND Code of Practice.

3. Find out which children in the classes you work with have additional needs. Do you feel confident in meeting their needs? What are their targets?

▶▶ **TAKING IT FURTHER**

The British Dyslexia Association, available at: www.bdadyslexia.org.uk.

Cremin, T and Arthur, J (2014) *Learning to Teach in the Primary School* (3rd edn). London: Routledge.

Goepel, J, Childerhouse, H and Sharpe, S (2014) *Inclusive Primary Teaching: A Critical Approach to Equality and Special Educational Needs*. Northwich: Critical Publishing.

The National Autistic Society, available at: www.autism.org.uk/.

The National Health Service (NHS) website has a range of useful pages:

NHS Attention Deficit Hyperactivity Disorder (ADHD), www.nhs.uk/conditions/Attention-deficit-hyperactivity-disorder/Pages/Introduction.aspx.

NHS Hearing Loss, www.nhs.uk/conditions/hearing-impairment/pages/introduction.aspx.

NHS Visual Impairment, www.nhs.uk/Conditions/Visual-impairment/Pages/Introduction.aspx.

REFERENCES

Bailey, R (2004) Gifted and Talented Education, in Soan, S (ed) *Additional Educational Needs: Inclusive Approaches to Teaching*. London: David Fulton.

Bearne, E and Kennedy, R (2014) Providing for Differentiation, in Cremin, T and Arthur, J (eds) *Learning to Teach in the Primary School* (3rd edn). London: Routledge.

Blamires, M (2004) Supporting the Inclusion and Achievement of Earners with Autistic Spectrum Disorders (ASD), in Soan, S *Additional Educational Needs. Inclusive Approaches to Teaching*. Abingdon: David Fulton Publishing.

Crossley, G (2013) Inclusion: Special Educational Needs, in Bold, C (ed) *Supporting Teaching and Learning*. Abingdon: Routledge.

DfE (2013) *National Curriculum*. [online] Available at: www.gov.uk/government/collections/national-curriculum (accessed July 2014).

DfE (2014) *Special Educational Needs (SEN) Code of Practice*. [online] Available at: www.gov.uk/government/uploads/system/uploads/attachment_data/file/342440/SEND_Code_of_Practice_approved_by_Parliament_29.07.14.pdf.

Equality for Human Rights Commission (2014) Glossary of Terms. [online] Available at: www.equalityhumanrights.com (accessed July 2014).

Hutton, M (2014) Classroom Difficulties of Children with Asperger Syndrome. [online] Available at: www.myaspergerschild.com (accessed July 2014).

NHS (2014a) Visual Impairment. [online] Available at: www.nhs.uk/Conditions/Visual-impairment/Pages/Introduction.aspx (accessed July 2014).

NHS (2014b) Hearing Loss. [online] Available at: www.nhs.uk/conditions/hearing-impairment/pages/introduction.aspx (accessed July 2014).

NHS (2014c) Attention Deficit Hyperactivity Disorder (ADHD). [online] Available at: www.nhs.uk/conditions/Attention-deficit-hyperactivity-disorder/Pages/Introduction.aspx (accessed July 2014).

Northcote, A (2014) Responding to Linguistic Diversity, in Cremin, T and Arthur, J (eds) *Learning to Teach in the Primary School* (3rd edn). London: Routledge.

Nutbrown, C and Clough, P (2006) *Inclusion in the Early Years*. London: Sage.

The National Autistic Society (2014) What Is Autism? [online] Available at: www.autism.org.uk (accessed July 2014).

Webster, R and Blatchford, P (2013) The Educational Experiences of Pupils with a Statement for Special Educational Needs in Mainstream Primary Schools: Results from a Systematic Observation Study. *European Journal of Special Needs Education* 28(4): 463–79.

6   The curriculum

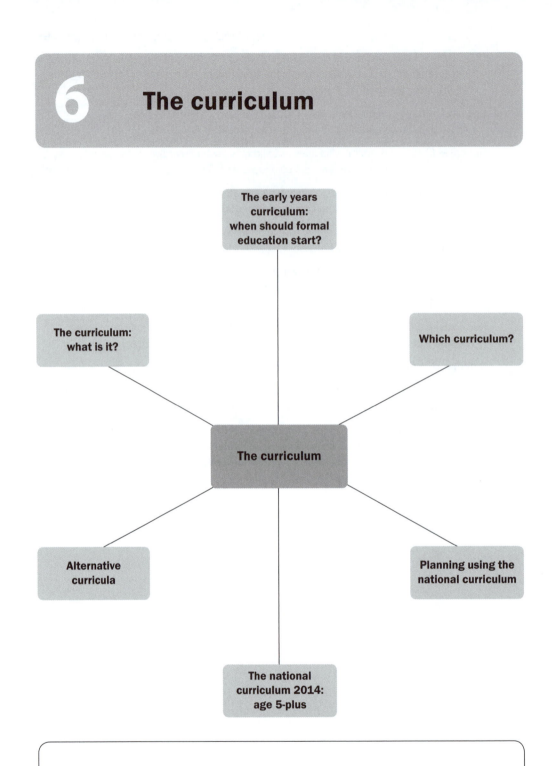

The early years curriculum:
when should formal
education start?

The curriculum:
what is it?

Which curriculum?

The curriculum

Alternative
curricula

Planning using the
national curriculum

The national
curriculum 2014:
age 5-plus

HLTA STANDARDS

This chapter links to the following HLTA standards (Training and Development
Agency for Schools (TDA), 2007, pp 97–98):

13: know how statutory and non-statutory frameworks for the school curriculum relate to the age and ability ranges of the learners they support;

14: understand the objectives, content and intended outcomes for the learning activities in which they are involved;

16: know how other frameworks, which support the development and well-being of children and young people, impact upon their practice.

INTRODUCTION

What is a curriculum? Is it a book that tells you what to teach – or is it something else? Where does it come from, who writes it and does it work? This chapter looks at who decides what goes on in our schools and why. It places the new Early Years Foundation Stage (EYFS) framework and the national curriculum (NC) in context, giving a background and useful step-by-step practical approaches to assist planning and delivery.

STARTING POINT

What is a curriculum for?

○ Is it for the child so he/she gets a rounded education?

○ Is it for 'society' so we can all be smarter and more prosperous as a nation?

Answer

Both. A curriculum should look at the individual child and the needs of society. For example, a curriculum that does not feature information and communications technology (ICT) or 'computing' would be seen as failing on both counts. The only question is what weight to place on individual (personalised learning) versus societal needs.

THE CURRICULUM: WHAT IS IT?

The Qualifications and Curriculum Authority (QCA) defined it as *'all the learning and other experiences that each school offers'* (QCA, 1999, p 2), while in its *Curriculum Guidance* the term is used to describe *'everything children do, see, hear or feel in their setting both planned and unplanned'* (QCA, 2000, p 2). Kelly states that the curriculum is the *'totality of the experiences the pupil has as a result of provision made'* (Kelly, 2004, p 8).

The *National Curriculum in England (2013) Framework* distinguishes between the *school* curriculum, which *'promotes the spiritual, moral, cultural, mental and physical development of pupils'*, and the national curriculum, which provides pupils with an introduction to the *'core knowledge that they need to be educated citizens'* (Blatchford, 2013, p 67). But when should the curriculum process begin?

> ### *Activity*
>
> What do you think is the absolute minimum children should be taught in our schools, and at what age? Spend a little time thinking about this. Most people would start with English and mathematics, but then what? How much priority should be given to music or PE, for example?

Duffy (2010) asks key questions for us all.

○ What do we believe is important for our children and why do we believe this? These are the values, aims and principles that our curriculum is based on.

○ When should we focus on particular learning experiences and how should we do this? This includes our understanding of children's likely patterns of development and our understanding of the processes involved in teaching and learning.

Any curriculum has to be fluid and responsive to changing needs:

> *We need a curriculum that can grow and evolve. The curriculum must be able to develop in response to changes in society and our understanding about how children learn – neither stand still – and neither should the curriculum.*
>
> (Duffy, 2010, p 98)

WHICH CURRICULUM?

There are many different kinds of schools in the UK. Scotland, Wales and Northern Ireland have their own *devolved* curricula, ie run locally. In Scotland, there is a *Curriculum for Excellence*, which is described as a *'coherent, flexible and enriched curriculum for learners from 3 to 18'* (Education Scotland, 2014). Responsibility for what is taught rests with councils and schools although they take national guidelines and advice into account. Similarly, in Wales the school curriculum is *'learner focussed, places an emphasis on skills development and ensures that it is appropriate for the specific needs of Wales'* (Welsh Government, 2014). Northern Ireland rewrote its curriculum in 1999 *'to meet the needs of young people, society, the economy and environment in the 21st Century'* and is run from Belfast (Northern Ireland Curriculum, 2014).

In England, the curriculum you will follow depends on the age of the children you are working with and the type of setting. There is an EYFS framework and a national curriculum. There are also different kinds of schools, such as those listed below, which legally do not have to follow the NC, although most have indicated they will.

- academy, or 'free schools';

- private (confusingly called public) schools;

- religious schools;

- grant-maintained schools;

- schools in Scotland, Wales or Northern Ireland.

(Department for Education (DfE), 2014a)

Activity

What kind of school/organisation do you work in? Check your school's prospectus or website. What does it say about the EYFS framework or the national curriculum?

THE EARLY YEARS CURRICULUM: WHEN SHOULD FORMAL EDUCATION START?

Question

What are the advantages and disadvantages of starting formal education before five years of age?

Answer

Advantages
- Gets children 'school ready'.
- Helps working parents.

Disadvantages
- Asks children to learn before they are physically and emotionally 'ready'.
- Institutionalises children too soon.

0–5 years

What is the *purpose* of 'education' between birth and five years, and is it fair to call it a curriculum? Duffy (2010) offers a useful overview. Should early years provision be:

- preparing children for school;

- day-care for working parents;

- stimulation for a developing brain;

- equal opportunities for women;

- cost savings for employers – so they can retain staff when they become parents;

○ reducing benefit bills for single parents, enabling a speedy return to work;

○ preventing developmental delay or juvenile crime?

(Duffy, 2010, p 8)

The early years curriculum is tied up with a swathe of legislation involving overall care of children. In 2014, the government published the *Statutory Framework* designed to improve the *'quality and range of education and childcare'* from birth to five years old. The *framework* is for everyone involved with childcare in whatever capacity, relating to nurseries, private nursery schools, pre-schools/playgroups and childminders. It replaced the old EYFS framework on 1 September 2014 and it:

○ sets the standards that all early years providers must meet to ensure that children learn and develop well;

○ ensures children are kept healthy and safe;

○ ensures that children have the knowledge and skills they need to start school.

(DfE, 2014b)

Early Years Foundation Stage (EYFS) 2014

The EYFS is not a curriculum as such but it carries a 'profile' that sets standards for the development, learning and care of children from birth to five. The EYFS Profile summarises and describes children's attainment at the end of the EYFS. It is based on ongoing observation and assessment and has a total of 17 Early Learning Goals (ELGs) in three prime and four specific areas of learning (DfE, 2014d), which can be seen in Tables 6.1 and 6.2.

Table 6.1 Three prime areas of learning (EYFS Framework)

ELGs: three prime areas of learning		
Communication and language	**Physical development**	**Personal, social and emotional development**
1. listening and attention 2. speaking 3. understanding	4. moving and handling 5. health and self-care	6. self-confidence and self-awareness 7. managing feelings and behaviour 8. making relationships

Table 6.2 Early Learning Goals: specific areas

ELGs: specific areas			
Literacy	**Mathematics**	**Understanding the world**	**Expressive arts and design**
1. reading 2. writing	3. numbers 4. shape, space and measures	5. people and communities 6. the world 7. technology	8. exploring and using media and materials 9. being imaginative

Children in the EYFS are assessed against criteria from:

○ birth–11 months;

○ 8–20 months;

○ 16–26 months;

○ 22–36 months;

○ 30–50 months;

○ 40–60 months +.

There is a great deal of information regarding expectations in the age ranges against the different areas. Early years practitioners are expected to make *'careful and detailed observations of progress'* (DfE, 2012).

The non-statutory guidelines *Development Matters in the Early Years Foundation Stage* (DfE, 2012) outline expectations in each age group in relation to:

○ a unique child: observing what a child is learning;

○ positive relationships: what adults could do;

○ enabling environments: what adults could provide.

Debate and analysis

Criticism comes from both ends of the political spectrum, saying the EYFS is either 'too much too soon' or not structured enough. Early Child Action (ECA) says the EYFS is *'prematurely imposed, developmentally inappropriate cognitive learning'* and *'facilitates the statutory imposition of unrealistic "normalising" developmental frameworks, including so-called "Early Learning Goals", on to the rich diversity of early experience'* (ECA, 2014). Others think the curriculum is not prescriptive enough. For example, education secretary Nicky Morgan MP announced that funding would be withdrawn from nurseries that do not *'promote British values'* (Adams, 2014a), while the current Ofsted chief Michael Wilshaw thinks middle-class prejudices stop all 0–5s having the chance to access quality childcare (Adams, 2014b). See Taking it further to follow the ongoing debate.

Activity

When should formal education begin in England? Should it start earlier, as in 'successful' Asian economies such as Singapore, or should England follow the example in Finland where formal education doesn't take place before 7 years of age? See the article *PISA Tests Damaging Education* by Peter Wilby, *The Guardian*, 6 May 2014 for a useful discussion.

THE NATIONAL CURRICULUM 2014: AGE 5-PLUS

In England the NC is a *'set of subjects and standards used by primary and secondary schools so children learn the same things. It covers what subjects are taught and the standards children should reach in each subject'*. These are outlined in Table 6.3. As mentioned, other types of schools such as academies and private schools don't have to follow the national curriculum. Academies must teach a broad and balanced curriculum including English, mathematics and science. They must also teach religious education (DfE, 2014a, NC Overview). The secondary curriculum is included to indicate progression.

Table 6.3 Structure of the new national curriculum

	Key Stage 1	**Key Stage 2**	**Key Stage 3**	**Key Stage 4**
Age	5–7	7–11	11–14	14–16
Year groups	1–2	3–6	7–9	10–11
Core subjects				
English	✓	✓	✓	✓
Mathematics	✓	✓	✓	✓
Science	✓	✓	✓	✓
Foundation subjects				
Art and design	✓	✓	✓	
Citizenship			✓	✓
Computing	✓	✓	✓	✓
Design and technology	✓	✓	✓	
Languages *		✓	✓	
Geography	✓	✓	✓	
History	✓	✓	✓	
Music	✓	✓	✓	
Physical education	✓	✓	✓	✓

* At Key Stage 2 the subject title for languages is 'foreign language'; at Key Stage 3 it is 'modern foreign language' (DfE, 2014b).

Context and analysis: an evolving national curriculum

At some point you will be asked to analyse viewpoints on the national curriculum, and the following extract provides some historical context.

> *From 1944 to the mid-1970s teachers enjoyed much freedom over what to teach and had effective control over the curriculum. Teachers in general were seen as having professional knowledge, integrity, expertise and were trusted with a high degree of autonomy. Generally, schools decided what was taught and were trusted to do so (Simon, 1991). Children earmarked for the 11+ went into grammar schools and were the main focus; the rest were taught 'the 3rs' of reading, writing and 'rithmetic with a view to going to the secondary modern school.*
>
> (Forrester and Garratt, 2012, p 72)

In the mid-1970s education became overtly political. The so-called 'Ruskin Speech' in 1976 for the first time linked economic failure to education. The country seemed to be 'in crisis', and part of the problem was schooling. The role of education was now to prepare young people for secondary school and then work. Teachers were criticised for selling the nation short and not teaching children properly (Whitty, 1990). It would not be the last time education and economic failure were linked.

The national curriculum arrived a decade or so later. The Education Reform Act (ERA) in 1988 created central control over educational content – the national curriculum was born. All state schools in England and Wales had to teach *core* subjects of English, mathematics and science and *foundation* subjects of art, geography, history, music, PE and technology plus a modern foreign language for children over 11 years. ICT came later. Standard Assessment Tests (SATs) were introduced and children were assessed against expected levels or 'standards' for their age. At the end of Key Stage 2 children were expected to have reached national curriculum level four.

The birth of school league tables followed quickly after. Inevitably, schools were compared with each other according to the 'best' grades, regardless of how deprived the surrounding area was (Gillborn and Youdell, 2000). The Office for Standards in Education (Ofsted) was created in 1992 to ensure standards were maintained and the national curriculum was being properly delivered. Some schools were 'failing' and were subsequently 'named and shamed' (Campbell, 2001).

The primary national curriculum underwent a review in 1997 with a focus on literacy and numeracy hours under the National Literacy Strategy and the National Numeracy Strategy respectively. In 2003, both of these strategies were amalgamated into the Primary National Strategy, and in 2006 this framework was relaunched as the *Primary Framework for Literacy and Mathematics*.

The Conservative–Liberal coalition took office in 2010 and the revision of the NC planned by Labour was put on hold so that the coalition could review it with a proposal as follows:

> *The new national curriculum will set out only the essential knowledge that all children should acquire, and give schools and teachers more freedom to decide how to teach this most effectively and to design a wider school curriculum that best meets the needs of their pupils.*
>
> (DfE, 2011)

The new national curriculum

The new national curriculum is underway. New statutory programmes of study and attainment targets were introduced in England from September 2014 for all year groups except Years 2 and 6. For those year groups, the new curriculum will take effect from September 2015 (DfE, 2013a). The headlines were made by a 'new tougher' slimmed-down version.

○ In mathematics, children will be expected to learn more at an earlier age – eg to know their 12-times table by the age of nine.

○ History will take a more chronological approach than under the old curriculum.

○ In English, pupils will learn more Shakespeare and there will be more importance placed on spelling.

○ The new computing (not ICT) curriculum will require pupils to learn how to write code.

○ In science, there will be a shift towards hard facts and 'scientific knowledge'.

(BBC News, 1 September 2014)

PLANNING USING THE NATIONAL CURRICULUM

Advice on planning using the new national curriculum is available on the DfE website. In the early stages of a career as a TA you will mainly be working under the direction of the teacher, but as your role grows in school then you may begin to take on aspects of planning yourself, so it is a good idea to understand where advice is to be found on what is suitable and age appropriate. There is considerable flexibility here, as schools are able to introduce content earlier than intended by the national curriculum documents, including in an earlier key stage if appropriate (see specific examples below) (DfE, 2013a). There are sections in the *Statutory Guidance Framework* (DfE, 2014b) on the overall structure of the NC and inclusion including the 'removal of barriers'.

Supporting the English curriculum: *Phonics*

Skills in the English language are *'essential to participating fully as a member of society; pupils who do not learn to speak, read and write fluently and confidently are effectively disenfranchised'* (DfE, 2013b). The DfE *Framework* (2014b) says English is a *'subject in its own right and the medium for teaching ... giving access to the whole curriculum ... and an essential foundation for success in all subjects'*. The sub-categories will be examined using *Key Stage 1 Phonics* as an example showing how the curriculum is at the same time distinct yet intertwined.

Spoken language

The NC programme of study (PoS) for English reflects the importance of spoken language in children's development across the whole curriculum – cognitively, socially and linguistically. Speaking and listening underpin reading and writing. Children therefore need to be exposed to a wide range of good-quality spoken language in order to develop their vocabulary and grammar, which are crucial in the development of their reading and writing skills. It is therefore essential that teachers focus on fostering pupils' confidence and competence in speaking and listening (English PoS, p 3).

Reading

Understanding that the letters on the page represent the sounds in spoken words is fundamental to all early reading skills. Fluent word reading involves both recognition and decoding skills, so children need to learn to recognise familiar printed words and should also develop the ability to work out the pronunciation of unfamiliar words quickly. This is why the NC emphasises the importance of phonics in the early teaching of reading (PoS, p 4).

Writing

If children are to write fluently they need to be able to spell quickly and accurately. This comes through knowing the relationship between sounds and letters and understanding the structure of words (morphology) (PoS, p 5).

Supporting the English curriculum (programmes of study)

Step one

Access the DfE (2013b) website: *English Programmes of Study: Key Stages 1 and 2: National Curriculum in England.* This is a comprehensive 88-page document that includes all statutory (ie compulsory) requirements and contains key appendices on graded spelling, vocabulary, grammar and punctuation with word lists from each key stage and the international phonetic alphabet (IPA). Become familiar with it: keep a link on your desktop or have a printed copy available. You will use this regularly. 'Own' it.

Step two

Find your school's planning 'proforma'. This will vary, but will have the key HLTA requirements of 'objectives, contents and learning outcomes' (TDA, 2007). It will look something like Table 6.4. Your 'box' is the Activity/Resources column where you explain what will happen.

Table 6.4 Example planning proforma

Date/time/ class	Curriculum reference	Objectives/ learning outcomes	Activity/ resources
	Progression/evaluation: What worked well/didn't work. What's next?		

Step three

Planning your Key Stage 1 phonics lesson – example. Consult your document. In the statutory requirements, students must *'use relevant strategies to build their vocabulary'* (English PoS, p 7).

In the non-statutory guidance (NSG) it states that students should be

> *taught at an appropriate level ... building on their oral language skills ... increasing their vocabulary ... working in groups of different sizes ... receiving constructive feedback on their spoken language and listening to ensure secure foundations ... into secondary school and beyond.*

(PoS, pp 7–8)

You are advised to follow this NSG at this stage in your career. The reason for phonics instruction is clear across the three components of English: Spoken Word, Reading and Writing.

Using the programmes of study, complete the planning sheet. The example in Table 6.5 looks at a Key Stage 1 lesson involving final consonant sounds. The relevant page numbers are contained for reference. Your involvement will be in the Activity/Resources column as you decide *how* to implement the relevant English PoS criterion.

Table 6.5 Key Stage 1 Phonics/spelling lesson

Date/time/ class	Curriculum reference	Objectives/ learning outcomes	Activity/resources
Yellow group 10.45–11.30 G2 Mr Graphem	Spelling (see English Appendix 1) Pupils should be taught to spell: ○ words containing each of the 40+ phonemes already taught ○ common exception words. *NC PoS (2013b) p 12*	**All** students will: correctly articulate end lateral consonant sounds /f/, /l/, /s/, /z/ and /k/ and apply decoding strategy – usually spelt as *ff, ll, ss, zz,* and *ck*, if they come straight after a single vowel letter in short words. **All** will 'sight read' exceptions: *if, pal, us, bus, yes.* **Most** will correctly spell *ff, ll, ss, zz and ck words.* **Some** will provide written context (sentence). Stretch: using multiple end consonant sounds in a sentence. *NC PoS (2013b) p 40*	The students will be given 'flashcards': *off, well, miss, buzz, back.* What do they say? Articulate the sound together, individually. Students follow/use 'Farm sounds' on *Pinterest.* Students will be encouraged to listen and guess the final /f/, /s/, /z/, /k/ and /l/ words being described. A rhyming word is given as a clue. Earn points! Students use whiteboards to spell/ sound out; compose /f/, /l/, /s/, /z/ and /k/ stories: '**off** we go or we will m**iss** the bus'
	Progression/evaluation: What worked well/didn't work. What's next?		

The final column, progression/evaluation, will indicate how well the outcomes were met and where you intend to go next. For example, some children may be ready to encode (write) their lateral consonant sounds in a composition, while others may need sight–sound reinforcement.

Regarding measuring attainment, the PoS says that by the end of each key stage, pupils are expected to *'know, apply and understand the matters, skills and processes'* specified in the relevant programme of study. In this example using *'relevant strategies to build their vocabulary'* (p 7), they will apply phonic knowledge and skills as the route to decoding words (p 10) and spell each of the *'40+ phonemes already taught'* (p 12). They will also write sentences by *'saying out loud what they are going to write about'* and compose *'a sentence orally before writing it'* (DfE, 2013b, pp 7–14).

This may seem an awful lot of work, but as you become familiar with the document and plan more regularly, the time spent on this will dramatically reduce.

Supporting the mathematics curriculum

Mathematics is important. The 2013 PoS says it is a *'creative and highly inter-connected discipline that has been developed over centuries [and is] essential for everyday life … providing a foundation for understanding the world, the ability to reason mathematically, an appreciation of the beauty and power of mathematics, and a sense of enjoyment and curiosity about the subject'*. It is not just numbers and calculations. There is an appendix (p 46) that looks at strategies for the 'four operations': addition, subtraction, multiplication and division (DfE, 2013c).

Through the mathematics curriculum it is intended that children will:

○ *'become fluent in the fundamentals of mathematics, including through varied and frequent practice with increasingly complex problems over time, so that pupils develop conceptual understanding and the ability to recall and apply knowledge rapidly and accurately;*

○ *reason mathematically by following a line of enquiry, conjecturing relationships and generalisations, and developing an argument, justification or proof using mathematical language;*

○ *solve problems by applying their mathematics to a variety of routine and non-routine problems with increasing sophistication, including breaking down problems into a series of simpler steps and persevering in seeking solutions.'*

(DfE, 2013c, p 3)

As with the English, follow a step-by-step approach, which may seem complicated at first but gets easier each time the action is performed. For example, suppose you have been asked to plan and prepare a Year 5 mathematics session on place value.

Step one

Access the NC PoS on the Department for Education website: DfE (2013c) *Mathematics Programmes of Study: Key Stages 1 and 2: National Curriculum in England*. Again you are advised to have a copy of this document and become familiar with its contents and general layout.

Step two

Access your school's proforma planning sheet – ask your teacher or mentor. It will look something like Table 6.6. Then fill in the details including 'your' box at the end.

Table 6.6 Year 5 Place value plan

Date/time/ class	Curriculum reference	Objectives/ learning outcomes	Activity/ resources
10.30–11.30 Compass group Mrs Angles Group/pair work	Place value (PV): Read Roman numerals to 1,000 (M) and recognise years written in Roman numerals. Identify the place value in large whole numbers. Continue to use number in context, including measurement; extend and apply their understanding of the number system. *NC PoS p 31*	The students select/ apply algorithms and 'translate' Roman numerals to 1,000 (M) and recognise years written in Roman numerals. The students will identify the value of each digit. Stretch: Ss will perform 10 'sums' with non-Arabic numerals eg L + XV =.	Ss research favourite movies and identify year of production using closing credits, eg *Shrek 2*. Students given unfamiliar movies (eg *Star Wars*) and do same. Ss pair up co-coach Roman addition sums; communication only in 'Roman'.
	Progression/evaluation: What worked well/didn't work. What's next? X correctly identified value of Roman numerals, found the task exciting but unchallenging. Pair work more fruitful (see display). **Next**: use Year 6 PoS (p 39) for extension with multiplication and division of Roman numerals to consolidate PV.		

The last section is important for continuity, planning and assessment: what do they know, what teaching and learning strategies worked and what next? You could go up and down the key stages or 'sideways' into the curriculum. As with English, you will be encouraged to reflect on the strengths and weaknesses, what could be built upon and encouraged as best practice.

There is flexibility in the NC (see mathematics example above) to 'dip in' to other key stages – above and below – for recap/extension work, as decisions about when to progress should always be based on the *'security of pupils' understanding and their readiness to progress to the next stage'*. Those who are not fluent with earlier material should be allowed to consolidate their understanding through further practice before moving on. It is also necessary to expand learning horizons for *'pupils who grasp concepts rapidly [and who] should be challenged through being offered rich and sophisticated problems before any acceleration through new content'*. There is a stipulated cross-curricular element in mathematics as an interconnected subject, which, although organised into 'distinct domains' in the PoS, should also be applied to science, ICT and other subjects (DfE, 2013c, p 3).

ALTERNATIVE CURRICULA

Parents who decide to educate their children themselves don't have to follow the national curriculum (see the Meeks in the case study) but they do need to inform the local authority and ensure they *'receive a full-time education from the age of 5'* (DfE, 2014a). There are also an estimated 80,000 children currently home-schooled in the UK (Walker, 2012).

Case study

The Meek family

In 2014 Amy and Ella Meek sold their house and embarked on a 2,000 mile road trip with their two children aged 11 and 9. They wanted a 'rounded education' for their children, which didn't involve 'regurgitating facts', and devised their own curriculum as follows.

Daily

Natural Fit – exercise/activity outdoors.

Thinking skills – task or morning discussion sparked by Thought for the Day on Radio 4.

Mathematics, reading, vocabulary

365 Project work – project to generate and publish 365 five-minute outdoor activities for children to try at home.

Weekly

Moral maze – discussion/debating skills.

Computer science – programming and app making.

Extended writing – for audience/purpose.

Watch and discuss a TED Talk (YouTube lectures in areas of technology, education, design)

News Round (up) – picking-up on topical news (UK and world)

Monthly

Book club – analysis/discussion/written response tasks to a book the children have studied.

Creative thinking project – problem finding and problem solving.

Media literacy skills – working towards creation and publication of podcasts, *vodcasts* and short videos.

'Big' adventure – weekend kayaking, canoeing, cycling, sailing, bushcraft.

(Topping, 2014)

Questions

○ What do you think about this curriculum?

○ Does it matter that the Meeks are teachers?

○ How practical is the road trip as an activity for everyone?

○ What are the benefits/disadvantages?

Answers

At first glance, it may seem any child's dream curriculum: for this family it will doubtless be an unforgettable experience. But for practical reasons the Meeks are in a unique situation. As teachers, they are able to support the curriculum in ways not often available to those outside education. Similarly, the decision to 'up sticks' and leave is not realistically open to the majority of the populace. Finally, the social aspects of schooling are denied. The Meeks would no doubt argue that dangers of bullying and 'regimentation' are avoided; however, schools teach more than the formal curriculum (see above) and 'life skills' that involve interaction with other people can only realistically be learned in a social environment.

▶▶ TAKING IT FURTHER

The 'official' view on curricula is given in the references. For discussions outside mainstream viewpoints, here are some educational considerations from the 'margins'.

ECA (2014) Speaking the Truth www.greenworld.org.uk.

Gatto, J T (2014) Classrooms of the Heart: Admit There Is No One Right Way to Grow Up Successfully (video) www.johntaylorgatto.com/.

Imaginative Inquiry (2014) Responses to the National Curriculum Review www.imaginative-inquiry.co.uk/2013/03/2014-national-curriculum-review.

International Primary Curriculum (IPC) (2014) Welcome to the IPC www.greatlearning. com/ipc/.

Pre-School Learning Alliance (2013) www.pre-school.org.uk.

The Good Schools Guide (2014) www.goodschoolsguide.co.uk.

REFERENCES

Adams, R (2014a) Nicky Morgan: Toddlers Must Learn British Values. *The Guardian*, 8 August. [online] Available at: www.theguardian.com/education/2014/aug/08/nicky-morgan-toddler-must-be-taught-british-values (accessed September 2014).

Adams, R (2014b) Ofsted Chief Accuses Middle-Class of Prejudice Against Early Years Teaching. *The Guardian*, 3 April. [online] Available at: www.theguardian.com/education/2014/apr/03/ofsted-chief-middle-class-prejudice-early-years-teaching (accessed September 2014).

BBC News (2014) *How Is the National Curriculum Changing?* [online] Avaliable at: www.bbc.co.uk/news/education-28989714 (accessed September 2014).

Blatchford, R (ed) (2013) *Taking Forward the Primary Curriculum: Applying the 2014 National Curriculum for KS1 and KS2*. John Catt Educational.

Campbell, R J (2001) The Colonisation of the Primary Curriculum, in Phillips, R and Furlong, J (eds) *Education Reform and the State – Twenty-Five Years of Politics, Policy and Practice*. London: Routledge Falmer, (pp 31–44).

DfE (2011) *The National Curriculum Relaunched*. [online] Avaliable at: www.gov.uk/government/news/national-curriculum-review-launched (accessed September 2014).

DfE (2012) *Development Matters in the Early Years Foundation Stage (EYFS)*. [online] Available at: www.foundationyears.org.uk/files/2012/03/Development-Matters-FINAL-PRINT-AMENDED.pdf (accessed September 2014).

DfE (2013a) *The National Curriculum in England Key Stages 1 and 2 Framework Document: September 2013*. [online] Avaliable at: www.gov.uk/government/uploads/system/uploads/attachment_data/file/335133/PRIMARY_national_curriculum_220714.pdf (accessed September 2014).

DfE (2013b) *English Programmes of Study: Key Stages 1 and 2: National Curriculum in England*. [online] Avaliable at: www.gov.uk/government/uploads/system/uploads/attachment_data/file/335186/PRIMARY_national_curriculum_-_English_220714.pdf (accessed September 2014).

DfE (2013c) *Mathematics Programmes of Study: Key Stages 1 and 2: National Curriculum in England*. [online] Avaliable at: www.gov.uk/government/uploads/system/uploads/attachment_data/file/335158/PRIMARY_national_curriculum_-_Mathematics_220714.pdf (accessed September 2014).

DfE (2014a) *The National Curriculum Overview*. [online] Avaliable at: www.gov.uk/national-curriculum/overview June 2014 (accessed September 2014).

DfE (2014b) *Statutory Guidance: National Curriculum in England: Framework for Key Stages 1 to 4*. [online] Avaliable at: www.gov.uk/government/publications/national-curriculum-in-england-framework-for-key-stages-1-to-4/the-national-curriculum-in-england-framework-for-key-stages-1-to-4 (accessed September 2014).

DfE (2014c) *Early Years Foundation Stage Handbook*. [online] Avaliable at: www.gov.uk/government/publications/early-years-foundation-stage-profile-handbook-2014 (accessed September 2014).

DfE (2014d) *National Curriculum Factsheet Update*. [online] Avaliable at: www.gov.uk/government/uploads/system/uploads/attachment_data/file/358070/NC_assessment_quals_factsheet_Sept_update.pdf (accessed September 2014).

DfE (2014e) *Statutory Framework for the Early Years Foundation Stage Setting the Standards for Learning, Development and Care for Children from Birth to Five*. [online] Avaliable at: www.foundationyears.org.uk/files/2014/07/EYFS_framework_from_1_September_2014__with_clarification_note.pdf (accessed September 2014).

Duffy, B (2010) The Early Years Curriculum, in Pugh, G and Duffy, B (eds) *Contemporary Issues in the Early Years* (5th edn). London: Sage.

ECA (2014) Speaking the Truth. [online] Available at: www.greenworld.org.uk/page371/page371.html (accessed September 2014).

Education Scotland (2014) The Curriculum. [online] Available at: www.educationscotland.gov.uk/thecurriculum/ (accessed September 2014).

Forrester, G and Garratt, D (2012) *Education Policy Unravelled*. Norwich: Continuum.

Gillborn, D and Youdell, D (2000) *Rationing Education – Policy, Practice, Reform and Equity*. Buckingham: Oxford University Press.

Kelly, A V (2004) *The Curriculum: Theory and Practice*. London: Sage.

Northern Ireland Curriculum (2014) Northern Ireland Curriculum. [online] Available at: www.nicurriculum.org.uk/about/ (accessed September 2014).

QCA (1999) *The National Curriculum: Handbook for Teachers in KS1 and 2 in England*. [online] Available at: www.educationengland.org.uk/documents/pdfs/1999-nc-primary-handbook.pdf (accessed September 2014).

QCA (2000) *Curriculum (Guidance for the Foundation Stage)*. [online] Available at: www.smartteachers.co.uk/upload/documents_32.pdf (accessed September 2014).

Simon, B (1991) *Education and the Social Order – British Education since 1944*. London: Lawrence & Wishart.

Topping, A (2014) School Trip: Teacher Parents Take Kids for Year of Learning on the Road. *The Guardian*, 3 September. [online] Available at: www.theguardian.com/education/2014/sep/03/teacher-parents-kids-year-learning-on-road (accessed September 2014).

Training and Development Agency for Schools (TDA) (2007) *Higher Level Teaching Assistant Candidate Handbook*. London: TDA. [online] Available at: www.education.gov.uk/publications/eOrderingDownload/TDA0420.pdf (accessed August 2014).

Walker, P (2012) Home-Schooled Children Face 'Postcode Lottery' of Official Support, Say MPs. *The Guardian*, 18 December. [online] Available at: www.theguardian.com/education/2012/dec/18/home-schooled-children-postcode-lottery (accessed September 2014).

Welsh Government (2014) The School Curriculum. [online] Available at: http://wales.gov.uk/topics/educationandskills/schoolshome/curriculuminwales/arevisedcurriculumforwales/?lang=en (accessed Sept 2014).

Whitty, G (1990) The New Right and the National Curriculum, in Flude, M and Hammer, M (eds) *The Education Reform Act. 1988: Its Origins and Implications*. London: The Falmer Press.

Wilby, P (2014) Academics warn international school league tables are killing 'joy of learning'. The Guardian, 6 May. [online] Available at: www.theguardian.com/education/2014/may/06/academics-international-school-league-tables-killing-joy-of-learning (accessed September 2014).

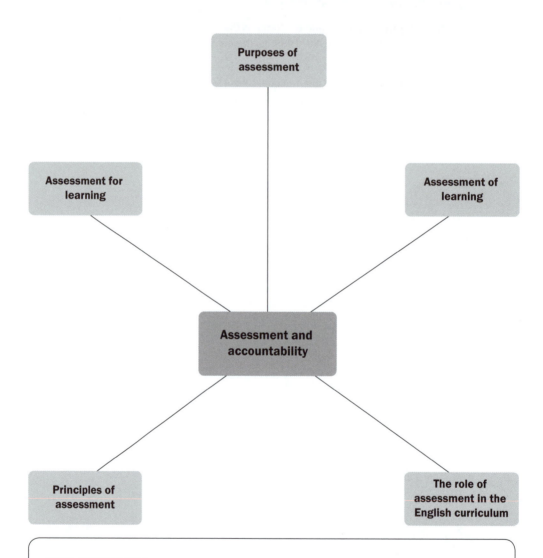

Purposes of assessment

Assessment for learning

Assessment of learning

Assessment and accountability

Principles of assessment

The role of assessment in the English curriculum

HLTA STANDARDS

This chapter links to the following HLTA standards (Training and Development Agency for Schools (TDA), 2007, pp 97–98):

22: monitor learners' responses to activities and modify approaches accordingly;

23: monitor learners' progress in order to provide focused support and feedback;

24: support the evaluation of learners' progress using a range of assessment techniques;

25: contribute to maintaining and analysing records of learners' progress.

INTRODUCTION

This chapter introduces key theories and principles underpinning assessment: how it informs planning, measures learning and contributes to quality systems. In relation to your role as a TA, you will therefore investigate:

○ key assessment requirements from early years to Key Stage 2;

○ theories, models and principles of assessment and feedback;

○ the importance of accurately monitoring, recording and reporting assessment results;

○ the need to modify assessment approaches to meet individual learning needs;

○ how assessment contributes to professional and school accountability.

STARTING POINT

○ What formal and informal assessments take place in your classes?

○ How do you support teachers with these assessments?

○ How do you support children in the assessment process?

PURPOSES OF ASSESSMENT

Assessment is a fundamental aspect of the English education system. League tables are based on results, which are used to compare local schools, and these also help Ofsted to prioritise school inspections (Swaffield and Dudley, 2010). Education ministers use assessment results to compare the efficacy of their education systems with international competitors as well as to justify policy changes (Robinson, 2014). You are therefore under pressure not just from concerned parents but also from your management to ensure your children achieve and exceed national minimum standards.

Assessment serves vital roles in our education system.

○ Formative assessment informs teachers and children of progress and future development needs.

○ Summative assessment provides recognition of achievement (or failure), usually at the end of a study period.

○ Assessment provides quantitative evidence for accountability purposes as well as to justify change.

○ Results are used to measure the performance of teachers, departments and education organisations (Swaffield and Dudley, 2010).

○ National systems are compared with international competitors in comparative studies and assessments such as the Programme of International Student Assessment by the Organisation of Economic Co-operation and Development (OECD, 2014).

As a teaching assistant (TA), you are involved in children's assessment at your school. Assessment is not just about completing formal tests – it's also often informal. For example, every time you ask a question, you're assessing the quality of a child's answer.

○ To what extent do they understand the concept?

○ Do I need to revisit this topic?

○ Is this work too easy? Could they be set more challenging tasks?

Formative (ongoing) assessment (such as the above) and summative (final) tests should therefore inform your planning when working with individuals and small groups. It should also form part of your communication with the classteacher. Assessment feedback communicates to the child their progress and future development needs. Your guidance should give them a clear understanding of how they can develop to meet these future targets, as well as why they are important. Assessment feedback should also be regularly communicated to parents, along with guidance about how they can contribute to the achievement of the child's learning objectives. This will most likely be the job of the classteacher, informed by your observations.

ASSESSMENT OF LEARNING

Assessment of learning measures children's abilities in a chosen area of knowledge or skill to provide a clear decision about their level of achievement. Such assessments may be baseline or summative. Baseline, or initial, assessments assess ability as a child starts their education at a school. Summative assessments pass final judgement on the achievements of individuals and groups at the end of a learning process (Swaffield and Dudley, 2010). An example of summative assessment is the end of Key Stage 2 national curriculum tests (commonly known under their acronym of American origin, SATs – Standard Assessment Tests). The baseline and summative assessment results can be compared to demonstrate how children have developed over the course of their study at a school. This can then be used as an indicator of the effectiveness of teachers and the organisation, even though external factors may also influence assessment results (Wilson and Kendall-Seatter, 2010).

Assessment and accountability: a careful balance?

Accountability is at the heart of the Department for Education's rationale for assessment:

> *Schools will be expected to demonstrate (with evidence) their assessment of pupils' progress, to keep parents informed, to enable governors to make judgements about the school's effectiveness, and to inform Ofsted inspections.*
>
> (DfE, 2014a, p 1)

Clearly, it is important for the children, teachers and the school to achieve high assessment results because such results can help to open up opportunities for further academic and eventually career development. To this end, it is important that children have experience of attempting summative tests before the actual event. This will help to reduce any potential stress and anxiety that they may suffer through the change of environment that such tests induce compared with their normal learning experiences. However, it's easy to assume that 'practice makes perfect', thinking that the more they experience taking tests, the better children will become at them. This can be particularly tempting if your school is under pressure to raise its assessment standards, but the Assessment Reform Group (1999, p 2) found that: *'There is no evidence that increasing the amount of testing will enhance learning.'* Bold (2011) further warns that excessive assessment practice narrows the curriculum, and Flórez and Sammons (2013) found that it detracts from the learning process as well as denying opportunities for broader social and emotional development. Endless repetition of tests quickly becomes boring and demotivates your children, leading to potential behaviour problems (Coffield and Williamson, 2012). Children can lose enthusiasm if tested excessively, which may lead to the very thing you have been working so hard to avoid – poor assessment results. Indeed, Bold (2011, p 157) argues that the current system of statutory assessment for children is counter-productive:

> *It is my belief that the current system of national testing has a negative impact on learning and teaching processes at key points in a child's educational history. Assessment should be a positive experience, enabling self-knowledge and growth rather than a process of labelling, categorising and the creation of a culture of failure. All too often the negative aspects of assessment processes override the recognition of the positive achievements of young people in our education system.*

Bold (2011) warns about the dangers of labelling children in terms of assessment on the grounds that potential demotivation may create a self-fulfilling prophesy, undermining the opportunity for the individual's ability to develop. Coffield et al (2004) further reject learning styles assessment labelling, finding insufficient evidence to support their use in education. Our understanding that ability is not fixed within individuals is a key reason for entering education in the first place as it is what motivates us to enhance the opportunities for our children to develop.

Question

To what extent do you agree/disagree with Bold's view? Why/why not?

Answer

A careful balance of learning experiences is important, where test preparation is a well-integrated, but not dominant, part of everyday learning, being one of the many school experiences from which children learn and develop:

What must be remembered is that pupils should be the ultimate beneficiaries of assessment. Where pupils are clear about what counts as progress and success, how assessments are made, and how they can use assessment feedback, then they can become more effective learners.

(Swaffield and Dudley, 2010, p 9)

ASSESSMENT FOR LEARNING

Assessment is therefore not just about measurement. Black and Wiliam (1998) used the term 'assessment for learning' (AfL) to provide focus on the forward-looking potential of assessment to inform and prioritise learner development, a concept summarised by Flórez and Sammons (2013, p 2):

Teachers who assess in this way are concerned not just to confirm and verify what their learners have learnt, but also to help their learners and themselves understand what the next steps in learning should be and how they might be attempted.

AfL can also be considered as *'assessment for teaching'* (Swaffield and Dudley, 2010) as it also helps to inform planning needs on both an individual and whole-class basis (see Figure 7.1). AfL therefore draws upon the constructivist/social-constructivist approaches to learning through its emphasis on active, participative and reflective learning based upon previous development and experience (Wilson and Kendall-Seatter, 2010). Flórez and Sammons's (2013) review of AfL found focusing on development rather than measurement may benefit learners through building positive self-esteem and developing personal responsibility for learning. Constructive feedback is therefore a key element of AfL.

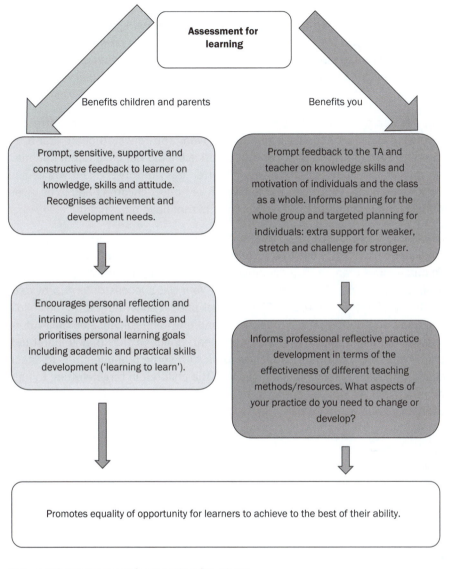

Figure 7.1 Assessment for learning flowchart
Adapted from Machin et al (2014)

AfL: learning through feedback

Some of you may remember receiving marks such as 'A+ Well done!', 'B– Must try harder!', or worse. Whatever your reaction to this – elated, baffled, dejected, or simply resigned – it is unlikely that such feedback prompted much in-depth reflection on the extent of your achievements and your future development needs. While such marks may help quantify achievement, they give the learner little help in terms of identifying and prioritising their future developmental needs. They do not provide an incentive to self-review past work to inform future development:

Informative and descriptive feedback is held to be more appropriate for a learning-centred perspective than the exclusive practice of marking work as right or wrong and giving just an overall mark. The latter is deemed to promote comparison and competition between students, and may in consequence damage their self-esteem if they get low scores compared with other students in their class.

(Flórez and Sammons, 2013, p 8)

According to research by Black and Wiliam (1998), feedback is one of the most effective means of enabling learning, especially when it is given, and reflected upon, just after the assessment. Therefore, this aspect of your practice should not be ignored, but must form a clear part of your learning strategies. It's often easy to forget this if you've just spent a long time marking homework, but to be truly effective, children need to be given time to carefully read and understand any comments that have been made.

Feedback can be given in a variety of ways, such as oral, written, pictorial or numerical or, ideally, in a combination of these to help reinforce understanding. Effective feedback is therefore much more than just a judgement of ability: *'Feedback needs to be specifically focused on the goals of the learning activity and the success criteria provided'* (Wilson and Kendall-Seatter, 2010, p 220). Feedback should accurately state the child's achievement and also 'feed forward' – prioritising and providing guidance on their future development needs, using objectives written in clear language that they understand. For example, written feedback could be followed up with some oral questions to check understanding. Bold (2011) recommends involving the children in target-setting to help check comprehension as well as enabling negotiation of meaningful and challenging objectives that are not over-ambitious.

Activity

- What input do your children have in setting objectives?

- How do you check that feedback and resulting objectives have been understood?

- How could you improve your practice in relation to these questions?

Swaffield and Dudley (2010) support the use of ipsative-referencing. This means that assessment and feedback, especially in formative assessment, should be based on your knowledge of the learner's ability. For example, a piece of work might score poorly in relation to the class, but this might still represent a real improvement for a struggling child. Grading alone would not recognise this development and could demotivate the child. Feedback should therefore be based not only on the quality of the work but also where this is in relation to the child's learning journey. However, this sensitivity needs to be balanced with inspiring high expectations in all learners. Ensure that tasks are always challenging relative to the individual ability of each learner to avoid children becoming stuck in a cycle of underachievement.

Results-based planning

As well as understanding individual learners' strengths and development needs, it is useful to know about any underlying trends within your class and school. This could be in terms of looking at specific areas of the assessment as well as the overall result; were there any sections or questions where the group tended to perform badly? Such areas could indicate either a need to revisit the syllabus in that area or a misunderstanding of the test rubric (the language used in the assessment). You should also consider whether any particular groups of children underperform. Organising results in terms of characteristics such as gender, ethnicity or pupil premium, for example, could help you to identify any particular groups that may need further support (Swaffield and Dudley, 2010).

PRINCIPLES OF ASSESSMENT

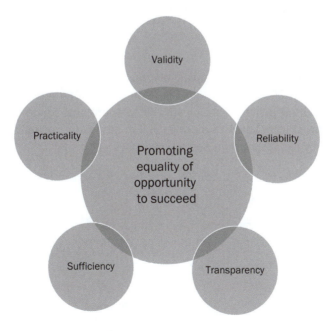

Figure 7.2 Key principles of assessment

Adapted from Machin et al (2014)

Validity

Assessment validity is the extent to which the assessment approach effectively evaluates the required knowledge, skills and abilities in relation to the stated aim of the test. Put another way, does the assessment do what it says on the tin?

Questions

Are the following valid assessments of reading ability?

1. You ask your children to read a story and then answer comprehension questions orally.

2. You give your children ten minutes to read a story and then answer comprehension questions in writing.

Answers

In both scenarios, your test now requires other skills as well as reading. Perhaps the children understand the text but cannot articulate this in writing or lack confidence in answering in front of the class (writing and speaking skills). Of course, there's nothing wrong with getting answers in such ways, but your test couldn't be considered a valid assessment of reading ability alone. Similarly, any test that is time-limited, as most formal assessments are, is effectively an assessment of children's ability to work quickly under pressure as well as of the subject focus.

Predictive validity

This reflects the extent to which assessments inform likely future results, though Swaffield and Dudley (2010) warn that while results may inform planning, they should never determine future achievement or solidify assumptions. Remember, a struggling child may suddenly start to succeed for any number of reasons, especially when you are supporting them by facilitating high aspirations.

Question

Your preparatory mock assessment gave much higher results than the actual summative assessment. Why might this have occurred?

Answer

It is likely that the two tests were conducted differently.

○ Was your mock assessment up to date and to the same standard as the exam?

○ Did you hold the preparatory test under exam conditions?

- ○ Was there a suitable environment for the assessments?

- ○ Were there any issues outside the classroom that may have distracted the children?

Consequential validity

Following on from this, the concept of *consequential validity* (Swaffield and Dudley, 2010) considers the appropriateness of how results are interpreted and used by interested parties. For example, to what extent are assessment results a valid indicator of the effectiveness of the school and its teachers? Are there other factors that may influence results?

Reliability

Swaffield and Dudley (2010, p 14) define reliability as:

> *the extent to which you can use the test on different occasions and with different pupils, and still be sure that the same things are being measured in the same way and to the same extent.*

Reliability is crucial for marking, where it concerns whether different markers would give the same grade for a piece of work. While this is easy for closed multiple-choice questions where an answer is either right or wrong, as often found with mathematics questions, open questions such as writing assessments are more problematic as criteria may be interpreted differently. You must therefore standardise your assessment marking with your colleagues so that you agree the standards of different pieces of work. This can be followed up by moderation of marked work to check that you are adhering to this standard consistently.

Reliability of assessment is also important for accountability as it enables comparisons within a whole cohort across the year, as well as in relation to previous years. This is used to give an indication of the relative success of teachers, schools or even the system as a whole, though such uses are not without controversy:

> *How is it that when we win more Olympic gold medals, the athletes receive OBEs and the coaches are praised for their preparation, but when schools improve their results we are accused of cheating, or are told that the exam was too easy?*
>
> (Anon, cited in Stewart, 2013)

Activity

To what extent do you agree/disagree with the above statement? Explain your answer in full.

Transparency

Transparency relates to the clarity of assessment processes, for children, parents, teachers and external organisations such as Ofsted. Children and parents need to be fully aware of the assessment purpose and processes involved, as well as how grades or marks are achieved:

> *Our collective classroom assessment challenge is to be sure students have the information they need, in a form they understand, and in time to use it effectively.*
>
> (Stiggins, 1994, cited in Swaffield and Dudley, 2010, p 9)

Transparency is therefore important in terms of adopting a fair marking process that teachers, parents and, increasingly with maturity, children, can understand. They should also be able to understand what a mark or grade means in terms of their achievement and future needs.

Activity

○ How effectively do you:

  – check children's understanding of assessment tasks?

  – check children's understanding of your feedback?

  – standardise and moderate assessments?

  – inform parents of assessment practice and discuss results with them?

○ In relation to the above, how do you evidence this practice?

○ Considering (1) and (2), what could you do better? Why and how?

Sufficiency

Assessments only sample part of a taught curriculum, otherwise they would become too long and impractical. Sufficiency, also referred to as content validity (Swaffield and Dudley, 2010), is therefore the extent to which an assessment is a reasonable reflection of the subject's syllabus knowledge, key concepts and skills.

Practicality

No assessment is perfect in relation to the above principles. Swaffield and Dudley (2010) note that the principles of reliability and validity can counter each other. For example, while a multiple-choice test may be reliable within a cohort in terms of producing 'right' or 'wrong' answers that are not open to the subjective interpretation of assessors, it may have questionable validity in terms of its ability to measure skills and deeper understanding. Conversely, creative writing exercises may be a valid assessment of writing ability, but are open to subjective interpretation of criteria, therefore bringing the reliability into question. Likewise, in general, the more reliable, valid and sufficient we attempt to make our assessment, the less practical and therefore more costly it becomes. Assessment is always a balancing act between striving towards these principles in order to create a fair assessment of our children's ability and practical considerations to use resources as efficiently as possible.

Activity

- o List the summative assessments that your children have to complete (eg the phonics screening test).

- o List how you formatively assess children (eg question and answer).

- o To what extent do you think each test and approach gives a fair judgement of your children's abilities? Why? Why not? Evaluate in relation to the principles of assessment outlined above.

- o Do any assessments appear to exclude any of your children? If so, how can this be avoided?

THE ROLE OF ASSESSMENT IN THE ENGLISH CURRICULUM

Assessment of learning is a crucial part of your role as a TA working in the English education system. Children's ability is formally measured throughout their time at school. Since the Education Reform Act (1988, cited in Whitty, 2008) standard national tests have been developed for all children from early years to Key Stage 4.

Assessment in the Early Years Foundation Stage (EYFS) curriculum

EYFS was introduced in 2008 to provide a broad framework to help early years providers deliver good learning and development opportunities for children (Tickell, 2011). Within this framework, early years assessment focuses on children's age-related progress in terms of health, development and 'school readiness' expectations (Ofsted, 2014a). While there is not currently an agreed definition of 'school readiness' (Ofsted, 2014b), the DfE's (2013) *Early Years Outcomes* provides guidance on expectations for children up to 60 months (5 years), with health expectations focusing on physical, social and emotional development. Education outcomes relate to English ability in terms of communication, language, reading and writing, mathematics, expressive arts and design and general understanding of the world. Each of these areas is broken into expected behaviours at differing stages of development and so can be adapted for individual assessment in relation to the children's peers as well as national expectations.

Statutory early years assessments

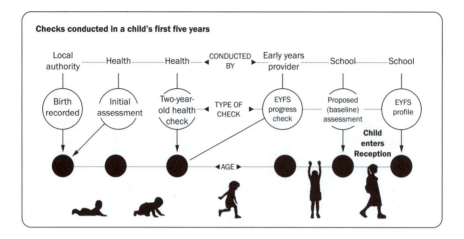

Checks conducted in a child's first five years

Figure 7.3 Statutory early years assessments flowchart
Source: Ofsted (2014a, p 14)

Ofsted (2014b) emphasises the importance of not just regularly informing parents of progress, but also working constructively with them and support services where specific needs or areas for development are identified. Therefore, parents should be made aware of developmental expectations for their children, their current progress and how identified needs can be addressed:

> *The best settings were acting to break any possibility of an inter-generational cycle of low achievement ... the most effective providers go out of their way to engage with parents who may themselves have had a bad experience of education.*
>
> (Ofsted, 2014b, p 12)

Tickell (2011) recommended increased parental responsibility and involvement in their child's progress, and this is also supported by Ofsted (2014b, p 15): *'It is parents who are ultimately accountable for a child's development.'* Ofsted notes that there is a strong correlation between poverty and low achievement and recommends that providers therefore need to give clear guidance on how parents can access support as well as what and how their children need to develop. Ofsted (2014a, p 10) provides an example of a successful integrated assessment process:

> *A children's centre nursery's meticulous assessment of children, which checked what they knew, identified any gaps in their skills and planned for their next steps, resulted in children making rapid progress and being confident and independent learners. An integrated health and early years review at 27 months of age, which involved the health visitor, the child's key worker, the child and the parent coming together to jointly review the child's health, development and learning, had a particularly positive impact on providing early intervention and support. Where there were concerns about a child's progress*

the integrated review process ensured that these were quickly addressed through referrals to relevant agencies.

Ofsted (2014a) suggests that online assessments may be useful as results can be easily shared between providers and parents, though it cautions that necessary safeguarding and data protection steps need to be in place regarding children's use of computers.

Ofsted recommends close co-operation during the transition to school, so that the child's learning is not disrupted by the move. Early years providers are expected to provide the school with a summative assessment of a child's abilities. However, at present there is no standard national baseline assessment on arrival into Reception, so Ofsted (2014a) has expressed concern about the quality and consistency of current practice. The DfE is therefore set to introduce standard assessments in 2016 (DfE, 2014b). Ofsted (2014b) argues that accurate baseline assessments are vital so that the school has a clear picture of a child's abilities and needs from their first day of transition, which means that learning approaches can be adapted to meet their needs straightaway. Indeed, they strongly recommend that pre-school providers and schools work closely together to moderate assessments (agree marking standards), share information about children during the transition stage and visit each other to share practice to minimise disruption.

Assessment in Key Stage 1

Information about the child's progress and development needs, based on the EYFS *Statutory Framework* (DfE, 2014c), is collated into a single report, the EYFS Profile (DfE, 2014d) at the end of every child's Reception year. The DfE introduced the new national curriculum for all maintained schools in September 2014 (DfE, 2014e). Reforms to the assessment process appear to represent both greater accountability measures and some new freedoms for schools. In terms of accountability, the forthcoming Reception baseline test and phonics check in Year 1 provide accountability through comparable standard national tests. Also, while Key Stage 1 assessment remains the teacher's responsibility, the DfE plans greater standardisation of practice. However, schools will not assess progress towards Key Stage 2 using the national curriculum levels system; the DfE now urges schools to develop or adapt their own means of measuring progress, though the summative national assessments at Key Stage 2 remain.

The phonics screening check

This is a short test in Year 1 for all maintained schools as well as other schools where this is specified in their funding agreement (DfE, 2014f). It comprises 20 words and 20 'pseudo' (made-up) words. Its stated purpose is to check children's ability to decode words through use of phonics – breaking down words into their component parts. This assessment has been criticised on several grounds. The government directive that synthetic phonics should be the only means of teaching reading for all children appears to contradict principles of tailoring learning to meet individual needs and promoting school freedom away from centralised control espoused in the government's education white paper, *The Importance of Teaching* (DfE, 2010). The test's use of pseudo words has been confusing for some children, especially if they are already higher level readers (UKLA, 2012). The pass/fail approach potentially demotivates children through 'labelling' them as failures, and, in terms of reliability, such a short test is also questionable (Hodgson et al, 2013).

Assessment in Key Stage 2

End the end of Year 6 (Key Stage 2) are the national curriculum tests, commonly known as SATs. Assessment involving creative writing has been replaced by an English grammar, punctuation and spelling test. As well as this there is an English reading test and mathematics test. All children take the test at levels 3–5, but, at the discretion of the headteacher, more-able children may attempt level 6 papers as well (STA, 2013).

Assessment to identify Special Educational Needs (and Disabilities) (SEND)

Just as assessment identifies the learning abilities and needs of all children, it is also a powerful means of identifying any SEND as soon as possible. This is essential so that appropriate support can be organised in order to enable the learner to achieve to the best of their ability as well as to enhance positive contributions to the class. Identifying such needs is at the heart of the SEND Code of Practice 0–25 (DfE, 2014g), which stresses the need to inform and involve parents and children as much as possible in the process through invitation to voice their views. Practitioners with all age groups are recommended to carefully observe and assess children to identify whether any developmental or learning issues may be related to SEND and to consider undertaking an Education, Health and Care (EHC) needs assessment. The Code cautions that not all such issues are necessarily due to SEND, giving the example that a child with English as an Additional Language may be achieving below expectations due to difficulties with learning a language. However, if a SEND is identified, this then usually informs a comprehensive EHC plan to promote multi-agency efficiency between these services. In addition to this, parents have the right to request an assessment if they consider that their child may have a SEND.

Making 'reasonable adjustments' for SEND children

The Equality Act (UK Government, 2010) expects education providers to make reasonable adjustments to support children's achievement. As well as adapting your planning, teaching and learning approaches to help meet their specific needs, you should also consider how assessment approaches may have to be adapted to give them the best opportunity to succeed. This does not mean that you should make the assessment 'easier' or compromise its aims, but that small changes in your method, negotiated with parents and the child, can help give SEND children a fair opportunity to demonstrate their ability in assessments that you have responsibility for marking. For national standardised assessments, the awarding organisation (AO) should be contacted as soon as the SEND is identified so as to enable special provisions in line with their guidance.

Questions

○ Do any of your children become stressed, upset or display challenging behaviour before or during an assessment?

○ How can you support your children to promote positive attitudes and behaviours during assessments?

Answers

Assessment, especially formal assessment, can be stressful for some children. This might be due to past failure or because of a change in the routine. Anxiety can be lessened if children have opportunities to practise assessment conditions beforehand. For example, prior to the SATs, you could gradually introduce elements of the actual assessment conditions during practice assessments. Rather than completing a whole assessment at once, this could at first be broken up into small sections, before gradually moving to longer periods as you get closer to the summative assessment. If a child's behaviour is linked to a SEND, then you should have reasonable adjustments in place to support them, from their EHC plan a well as guidance from the awarding body.

 # Check your understanding

Review your current assessment approaches and methods:

1. Do any groups of children underperform in relation to others?

2. How do you know this (from data)?

3. What plans are being implemented in your setting to support these children?

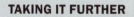 **TAKING IT FURTHER**

BBC (2012) *Do Schools Make a Difference?* Analysis BBC Radio 4 Podcast. www.bbc.co.uk/programmes/b01b9hjs (accessed May 2014).

DfE School Performance Tables. www.education.gov.uk/schools/performance/ (accessed August 2014).

RAISEonline *Reporting and Analysis for Improvement through School Self-Evaluation.* www.raiseonline.org/login.aspx?ReturnUrl=%2f (accessed September 2014).

REFERENCES

Assessment Reform Group (1999) Beyond the Black Box. [online] Available at: www. nuffieldfoundation.org/sites/default/files/files/beyond_blackbox.pdf (accessed September 2014).

BBC (2014) *The Educators – Sir Ken Robinson* BBC Radio 4. [online] Available at: www.bbc. co.uk/programmes/b04d4nvv (accessed September 2014).

Black, P and Wiliam, D (1998) *Inside the Black Box: Raising Standards Through Classroom Assessment*. London: King's College.

Bold, C (ed) (2011) *Supporting Learning and Teaching* (2nd edn) Oxon: Routledge.

Coffield, F, Moseley, D, Hall, E and Ecclestone, K (2004) *Should We Be Using Learning Styles? What Research Has to Say About Practice*. Trowbridge: Cromwell Press.

Coffield, F and Williamson, B (2012), *From Exam Factories to Communities of Discovery*. London: Institute of Education.

DfE (2010) *The Importance of Teaching: The Schools White Paper*. London: DfE. [online] Available at: www.gov.uk/government/publications/the-importance-of-teaching-the-schools-white-paper-2010 (accessed September 2014).

DfE (2013) *Early Years Outcomes*. [online] Available at: www.gov.uk/government/ publications/early-years-outcomes (accessed September 2014).

DfE (2014a) *Assessment Principles* London: DfE. [online] Available at: www.gov.uk/ government/uploads/system/uploads/attachment_data/file/304602/Assessment_ Principles.pdf (accessed August 2014).

DfE (2014b) *Reception Baseline Assessment.* [online] Available at: www.gov.uk/government/ policies/making-schools-and-colleges-more-accountable-and-giving-them-more-control-over-their-budget/supporting-pages/reception-baseline-assessment (accessed September 2014).

DfE (2014c) *Early Years Foundation Stage Framework.* [online] Available at: www.gov. uk/government/publications/early-years-foundation-stage-framework–2 (accessed September 2014).

DfE (2014d) *Early Years Foundation Stage Profile 2014* London: DfE. [online] Available at: https://www.gov.uk/government/publications/early-years-foundation-stage-profile-handbook-2014 (accessed September 2014).

DfE (2014e) *National Curriculum and Assessment: Information for Schools.* [online] Available at: www.gov.uk/government/publications/national-curriculum-and-assessment-information-for-schools (accessed September 2014).

DfE (2014f) *Statutory Phonics Screening Check*. [online] Available at: www.gov.uk/ government/policies/reforming-qualifications-and-the-curriculum-to-better-prepare-pupils-for-life-after-school/supporting-pages/statutory-phonics-screening-check (accessed September 2014).

DfE (2014g) *Special Education Needs Disability Code of Practice 0–25*. London: DfE. [online] Available at: www.gov.uk/government/publications/send-code-of-practice-0-to-25 (accessed 2014).

Flórez, M and Sammons, P (2013) *Assessment for Learning*. Reading: CfBT. [online] Available at: www.cfbt.com/en-GB/Research/Research-library/2013/r-assessment-for-learning-2013 (accessed September 2014).

Hodgson, J, Buttle, H, Conridge, B, Gibbons, D and Robinson, J (2013) *Phonics Instruction and Early Reading: Professional Views from the Classroom.* Sheffield: NATE. [online] Available at: www.nate.org.uk/index.php?page=8&paper=11 (accessed October 2014).

Machin, L, Hindmarch, D, Murray, S and Richardson, T (2014) *A Complete Guide to the Diploma in Education and Training.* Northwich: Critical Publishing.

OECD (2014) *Programme for International Student Assessment.* [online] Available at: www.oecd.org/pisa/aboutpisa/ (accessed September 2014).

Ofsted (2014a) *The Report of Her Majesty's Chief Inspector of Education Children's Services and Skills – Early Years.* Manchester: Ofsted. [online] Available at: www.gov.uk/government/uploads/system/uploads/attachment_data/file/386504/Ofsted_Early_Years_Annual_Report_201213.pdf (accessed January 2015).

Ofsted (2014b) *Are You Ready? Good Practice in School Readiness.* Manchester: Ofsted.

Robinson, K (2014) The Educators (programme 1) BBC Radio 4, first broadcast 1 September 2014. [online] Available at: www.bbc.co.uk/programmes/b04d4nvv (accessed 24 November 2014).

Stewart, W (2013) Is There No Way up for Results? *Times Educational Supplement,* 24 April.

STA (2013) *Key Stage 2 Tests: An Overview.* [online] Avaliable at: www.gov.uk/government/publications/key-stage-2-tests-an-overview (accessed September 2014).

Swaffield, S and Dudley, P (2010) *Assessment Literacy for Wise Decisions* (3rd edn). London: Association of Teachers and Lecturers.

Tickell, C (2011) *The Early Years: Foundations for Life, Health and Learning – an Independent Report on the Early Years Foundation Stage to Her Majesty's Government* DfE: London. [online] Available at: www.gov.uk/government/publications/the-early-years-foundations-for-life-health-and-learning-an-independent-report-on-the-early-years-foundation-stage-to-her-majestys-government (accessed September 2014).

Training and Development Agency for Schools (TDA) (2007) *Higher Level Teaching Assistant candidate handbook.* London: TDA. [online] Available at www.education.gov.uk/publications/eOrderingDownload/TDA0420.pdf (accessed January 2015).

UK Government (2010) *The Equality Act 2010.* [online] Available at: www.legislation.gov.uk/ukpga/2010/15/pdfs/ukpga_20100015_en.pdf (accessed September 2014).

UKLA (2012) *UKLA Analysis of Schools' Response to the Year 1 Phonics Screening Check.* Leicester: UKLA.

Whitty, G (2008). Twenty Years of Progress? English Education Policy 1988 to the Present. *Education Management Administration Leadership,* 36(2): 165–84.

Wilson, V and Kendall-Seatter, S (2010) *Developing Professional Practice 7–14.* Harlow: Longman.

8   Teamworking

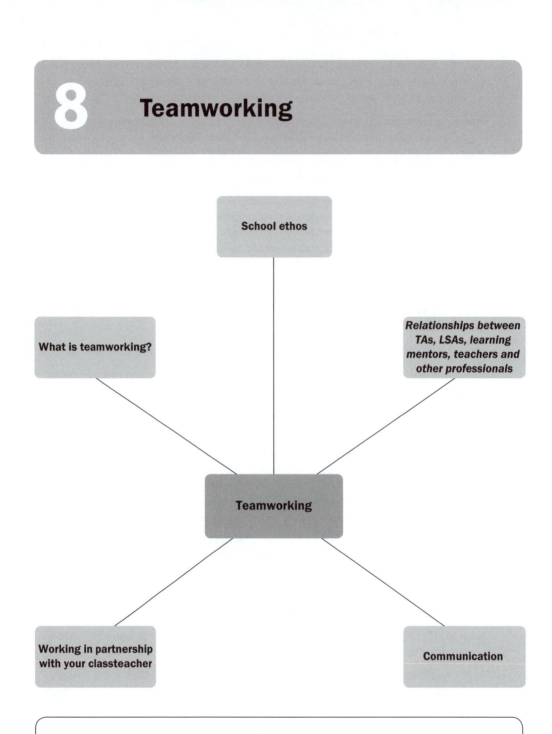

- School ethos
- What is teamworking?
- Relationships between TAs, LSAs, learning mentors, teachers and other professionals
- Teamworking
- Working in partnership with your classteacher
- Communication

HLTA STANDARDS

This chapter links to the following HLTA standards (Training and Development Agency for Schools (TDA), 2007, pp 96–97):

3: demonstrate the positive values, attitudes and behaviour they expect from children and young people;

4: communicate effectively and sensitively with children, young people, colleagues, parents and carers;

6: demonstrate commitment to collaborative and co-operative working with colleagues;

26: use effective strategies to promote positive behaviour;

31: advance learning when working with whole classes without the presence of the assigned teacher;

32: organise and manage learning activities in ways that keep learners safe;

33: direct the work, where relevant, of other adults in supporting learning.

INTRODUCTION

This chapter examines the area of teamworking. In particular, it will consider how teaching assistants (TAs) work in partnership with the classteacher and the relationships that exist between TAs, learning support assistants (LSAs), learning mentors, teachers and other professionals.

STARTING POINT

○ What do you understand by the term teamwork?

○ Which adults do you work with?

○ Do you know the names of all of the adults who work in the same classroom/s as you do?

WHAT IS TEAMWORKING?

Teamwork refers to two or more individuals working collaboratively together in order to achieve a set of objectives. Individuals use and combine their skills with other members of the team in order to work efficiently and effectively towards positive outcomes. Research by Groom and Rose (2005) found that the ability to work as a member of a team was an attribute sought by schools when recruiting new staff, and seen as being *'crucial for children to receive the best learning experience possible'*.

> *Individual commitment to a group effort – that is what makes a team work.*
> (Vince Lombardi, on BrainyQuote.com: www.brainyquote.com/quotes/
> quotes/v/vincelomba129818.html [accessed 29 July 2014])

Many schools now employ a range of professionals to work with and alongside a teacher in and outside of the classroom. This includes TAs, LSAs, SEN assistants, SENCOs, classroom volunteers and administrators. All work to provide an inclusive and support-ive school environment that provides a climate for children to thrive and achieve their full potential. Knowing the names of the people that you work with can help you build and maintain collaborative working relationships with them.

Roles and responsibilities

Question

What are your roles and responsibilities within the classroom and within the school?

Answer

You might have included some of the following:

o getting the classroom ready for lessons;

o listening to children read, reading to them or telling them stories;

o helping children who need extra support to complete tasks;

o helping teachers to plan learning activities and complete records;

o supporting teachers in managing class behaviour;

o supervising group activities;

o looking after children who are upset or have had accidents;

o clearing away materials and equipment after lessons;

o helping with outings and sports events;

o taking part in training;

o carrying out administrative tasks.

You may also be involved in:

o working alongside teachers to support learning activities;

o helping to plan lessons and prepare teaching materials;

o acting as a specialist assistant for particular subjects;

o leading classes under the direction of the teacher;

o supervising other support staff.

National Careers Service (2012, p 2)

Question

Do you know what the roles and responsibilities are of the teacher, other support workers, volunteers or any other adults who work in the same classroom/s as you do and/or are involved in the children's well-being?

Answer

One of your roles is to have a good understanding of what it is the teacher does so that you know how best to support them, for example knowing when they will be out of the classroom during the school day to do preparation, planning and assessment (PPA). You should also have an awareness of the duties of the SEN, SENCO, LSAs and others employed in the school.

As well as knowing what your own roles and responsibilities are, having some knowledge of your colleagues' roles and responsibilities ensures that you can *'direct the work, where relevant, of other adults in supporting learning'* (HLTA standard 33 – TDA, 2007, p 97). Getting to know the right person to speak to is a communication strategy as well as a good time-management technique. Building working relationships is crucial for developing a positive and enhancing learning climate.

WORKING IN PARTNERSHIP WITH YOUR CLASSTEACHER

Clarity about roles and being able to communicate with those you work with is important because, according to research carried out in 2003 by Cremin, having other adults to help out in the classroom does not necessarily enhance children's learning experiences. Neither does it necessarily provide more time for the teacher to spend with the children. In fact, it can have the opposite effect and result in a teacher spending less time with the children. The type of support required and given by TAs and other adults working in a classroom needs to be carefully thought out and planned or, to use two idiomatic expressions, rather than many hands making light work it could be a case of too many cooks spoiling the broth.

Activity

○ Does the classroom teacher do all, or any, of the following?

- take account of your role in the class session when planning the curriculum and preparing the resources to be used;

- use learning strategies that ensure a clearly defined role for you to be effectively engaged with the children/child;

- talk with you about the effectiveness of lessons;

- give you feedback on your input.

○ Do you report on the progress of individual children to the teacher?

If a teacher feels confident about the quality of help and support that they receive from you or other suitably qualified professionals then they are more likely to give you (or others) tasks that can free them up for PPA. In order for lessons to be consistently outstanding, it is important that teachers do their best and also facilitate the same standard from their team.

Question

To what extent do you and your teacher discuss the following? What input do you have?

○ lesson planning;

○ classroom rules;

○ behaviour strategies.

Answer

Engaging in discussions with the teacher and any other adults working in the classroom helps to promote a positive classroom climate where children feel safe and secure. A positive classroom climate provides optimal opportunities for learning within a motivational, fair and supportive environment – all of which Hay McBer (2000) considers crucial for the promotion of positive learning encounters for children. Furthermore, having some input in the planning process means that you should be more prepared and able to *'advance learning when working with whole classes without the presence of the assigned teacher'* (HLTA standard 31 – TDA, 2007, p 97). Whether the teacher is in the classroom or not, your role, while also important, is different from theirs.

Question

How do you differentiate between the teacher's role and your own?

Answer

You have an important role to play in developing children's learning but it is complementary to and not the same role as that of a teacher.

 **Case study**

Raising standards

Teachers and HLTAs are not interchangeable. The fact that HLTAs may be working with whole classes for some of the time does not make them substitutes for when children need a qualified teacher, bringing the extra range, experience and complexity of understanding reflected in their greater professional training. The use of HLTAs to undertake 'specified work' is not intended to worsen child–teacher ratios but should improve child–adult ratios.

When you are discussing your role and duties with the classroom teacher you should be identifying ways in which that role can be extended in order to raise standards, enhance children's learning experiences and add support to the improvement of the whole school.

Woodward and Peart (2006, pp 8–11)

Question

How can you help the teacher to raise standards?

Answer

By carrying out the tasks designated to you proficiently and enthusiastically, you are freeing up the teacher's time to do other educational duties.

Case study

Yvonne

I started to work at the primary school about six months ago. Two of my own children were at this school so I already knew many of the teachers, parents and children. I work with an Early Years Foundation Stage teacher and, as I am working towards my HLTA status, I have the opportunity to be involved in some of the teaching. If the teacher needs to go out of the class for a short while I become responsible for the smooth running of the class and the children's well-being. It wasn't always like this as when I first started I got the impression that the teacher didn't like anyone in the class with her and was, I thought, a little frosty with me when I used my initiative or if a child came to me instead of her. Now it's different; I think that the teacher appreciates the PPA time that she has and trusts me to do a good job under her direction.

Questions

- Why might the teacher have been frosty with Yvonne when she used her initiative?

- Why would the teacher be frosty with Yvonne because a child went to her?

- What changed this situation?

Answer

The teacher needed to get to know Yvonne and to develop a trusting working relationship with her. When Yvonne used her initiative the teacher may have been concerned that Yvonne did not have enough experience to carry out tasks any differently than had been outlined. Or the teacher may have considered that she had not given Yvonne sufficient direction to allow her to carry out tasks in a manner conducive to the children's learning experiences. Another reason for the teacher's response might be a real or perceived shift in the power dynamics in the classroom whereby the teacher may have felt her status was threatened when children went to Yvonne instead of her. She may also have been concerned that Yvonne wasn't yet demonstrating sufficient skills to *'organise and manage learning activities in ways which keep learners safe'* (HLTA standard 32 – TDA, 2007, p 97) and that she wouldn't know what to do about any request made to her by the children. Building a close and trusting working relationship takes time.

Activity

What do you do, or what could you do, to develop a strong working relationship with your classteacher? Think specifically about areas of strength and areas for development.

Case study

Ben

I have always felt like a valued member of the staff and I like to think that I make useful contributions to the team. I sometimes take a whole-class session for literacy, which I really enjoy. I work mostly with children in Key Stage 1, but occasionally I am asked to go and support a teacher in Key Stage 2. In the Key Stage 1 class there are also two SEN support workers; so with four adults and 30 children the classroom is full and needs to be well managed. The teacher plans the work but, as much as time permits, discusses each session with me and the SENs at some point during the day. This gives us all an opportunity to discuss any issues and to talk to each other about how good (or not so good) the sessions were. Mostly the sessions are good; Ofsted says so and so do the parents. Importantly, all of the children seem happy.

Activity

In the case study above, identify the significant factors that are influencing the positive classroom climate that Ben outlines.

Collaborative teamwork is crucial to the classroom climate and a child's learning. In the case study above, there are 30 children, some of whom require the support of a SEN support worker. With such a large class, it is likely that there are always going to be some children who are not paying attention to the teacher or who are easily distracted and misbehave. As a TA you can support the teacher by *'using effective strategies to promote positive behaviour'* (HLTA standard 26 – TDA, 2007, p 97), for example, by using a range of non-disruptive tactics (eg a look, a gesture, quiet word or repetition of task requirements) to ensure that all children are listening or engaged in any work set. (For more information about behaviour, see Chapter 3.)

RELATIONSHIPS BETWEEN TAs, LSAs, LEARNING MENTORS, TEACHERS AND OTHER PROFESSIONALS

Everyone at the school where you work needs to make a contribution as a team member. All have a responsibility to make sure that the school has a safe, secure and inclusive learning environment where children are able to thrive socially and academically. Alongside the teaching staff, many schools now employ trainee teachers, TAs and support workers as well as volunteers to help with classroom and extra-curricular activities. As a TA you need to be able to *'demonstrate commitment to collaborative and co-operative working with colleagues'* (HLTA standard 6 – TDA, 2007, p 96). You need to make sure that you carry out your roles and responsibilities efficiently, enthusiastically and in a timely manner. You should, if you are able, also be willing to give the teacher and any other adults in the class a little extra help when you can and as you see is necessary. This is not only good for the children's well-being but also helps to cement good working relationships; as does, on a more personal level, showing an interest in your colleagues and asking them about their hobbies and interests. But a note of caution – be interested, not nosy – do not push for a response. Importantly, remember to thank people for the help, guidance and support that they give to you; give them the credit, where necessary, for any jobs done. Overall, be aware of the roles of those with whom you work as well as any strengths and skills that they have; use their strengths and where possible support their weaknesses. Building trusting working relationships is important, as Coleman

(1988, p 100) contends that a team where trust between each of the members exists is *'able to accomplish more than a comparable group without trust'*.

Lave and Wenger (2003) call groups of people who come together with a common purpose a community of practice, which they describe as having:

o   mutual engagement;

o   joint enterprise;

o   shared repertoire.

Belonging to a community of practice can give you and your colleagues the opportunity to share ideas and give feedback to each other. Before you can do this, though, you need time to get to know each other and to understand what it is the teacher wants you and the other team members to do.

Developing a team takes time. In 1965, Bruce Tuckman, Professor Emeritus of Educational Psychology at Ohio State University, developed a model that is still regularly used to describe the essential stages of team development.

Forming: Individuals come together and gradually get to know each other.

Storming: Individuals vie for their position and their role in the group.

Norming: Individuals come together and work as a collective, positions are accepted and group norms are established.

Performing: Individuals carry out tasks in order to reach goals and targets.

Adjourning: The team, for a variety of reasons, disbands.

Your school, like all other organisations, wants the teams that exist in the school to *perform* – this is crucial for the well-being and successful outcomes of the children as well as the overall efficiency of the school, and not forgetting, of course, the requirements of Ofsted. The school where you work will most likely have had procedures in place to welcome you and to induct you into your role and your place in the school. Your line manager, the classroom teacher and any other individuals that you work with will have been keen for you to establish your place within the team quickly.

According to Belbin (1993), successful teams usually consist of individuals with differing attributes, summarised in Table 8.1. Belbin contends that the most efficient and effective teams have individuals with the skills and attributes of one or more of those shown, and that there are no good or bad roles; all have an important part to play in the success of the team.

Table 8.1 Belbin's team roles

Team role	Strengths	Weaknesses
Plant	Creative, imaginative, unorthodox, problem solver	Not good at communicating with less creative team members
Resource investigator	Enthusiastic, communicative, outgoing, negotiator	Quickly loses enthusiasm

Team role	Strengths	Weaknesses
Co-ordinator	Confident, able to get others to work together, sees what is necessary to get the job done	Can be coercive and seen as indifferent
Shaper	Outgoing, challenges, finds solutions to problems, motivated, achievement-driven, dynamic	Inclined to become irritated and annoyed
Monitor-evaluator	Strategically minded, seeks all options and makes accurate judgements	Lacks incentive and inspiration
Teamworker	Social, seeks a collective group ethos, good listener, averts and avoids confrontation, wants to maintain the status quo	Can be indecisive/sits on the fence
Implementer	Loyal, reliable, practical, efficient	Can be uncompromising, especially with new ideas
Completer/finisher	Conscientious, keeps going until a task is completed, diligent, meets deadlines	Easily stressed and can find it difficult to delegate
Specialist	Focused, motivated, knowledgeable and/or skilful in a specific area	Contributions limited to what they know and is of interest to them

Although the efficiency and effectiveness of any team, including any that you belong to, relies on *groupthink*, ie shared understandings, one of the downsides is that negative as well as positive groupthink can occur. Groupthink, according to Janis (1982), occurs for a variety of reasons. For example, individuals within a team (usually the less confident) may fail to voice alternative views or courses of action to those made by the more assertive, stronger, more animated group members. As another example, if team members are very similar to one another there is likely to be an abundance of some of the skills and a scarcity of some of the others; therefore the group may share common thinking ground. Groupthink can also occur when a team has a charismatic leader who is able to use this trait (consciously or unconsciously) to influence the team. Stress can also reduce individual members of a team to groupthink.

COMMUNICATION

A good team is made up of people who communicate with each other. Effective communication between you, the classteacher, other support staff and management is essential for the success and well-being of the children and of the school.

Activity

○ How much time each day do you think that you spend:

- supporting the teacher;

- – supporting/working with support staff;
- – on other tasks, eg administration, break duty?
- o Each of the above roles involves you working with another member of staff; therefore good communication skills are required.

Communication between you, the teacher and others within the school might be formal, informal, verbal or written. In every case, you need to ensure that you are:

- o respectful of others;
- o supportive;
- o clear about what you want to say;
- o non-judgemental;
- o attentive and listen carefully to (or read) what others have to say;
- o using non-verbal body language that supports your verbal language (what you say is what you mean).

Formal verbal or written communication might take the form of staff meetings, sharing and contributing to the staff handbook and face-to-face discussions. Informal communication might take the shape of routine conversations, notes and emails.

Whatever method of communication you are using with those that you work with, you should always show respect for each individual. Forgetting to include someone in a communication trail or forgetting to thank someone for something that they have done can make them feel unvalued. Also, don't be tempted to join in negative conversations about others in the staffroom as this can only lead to upset and a dysfunctional team. Problems with communication and with the team can ultimately affect the children's learning experiences and the overall success of the school. It is therefore essential that you are able to *'communicate effectively and sensitively with children, young people, colleagues, parents and carers and the wider children's workforce'* (HLTA standard 4 – TDA, 2007, p 96).

Activity

Consider a group of children or an individual child you are working with regularly.

- o Who do you need to communicate with in order to support the children/ child?
- o Which methods of communication do you use when seeking advice and support regarding the children/child from the teacher or support staff (eg face-to-face, email, formal/informal meetings)?
- o How could you improve your method of communication?
- o How could methods of communication be improved in your school?

A collective group of individuals is not necessarily a team. If you don't communicate with each other, or if, when you do, you simply engage in gossip, you are not a team. Teams have purposeful conversations that lead to a common goal; as the cliché goes, there is no 'I' in team.

SCHOOL ETHOS

One of the structures that Ofsted looks for when inspecting and making a judgement about a school is *'the extent to which leaders and managers have created a positive ethos in the school'* (Ofsted, 2014 framework, pp 18–19).

An ethos is defined as *'The characteristic spirit of a culture, era or community as manifested in its attitudes and aspirations'* (*Oxford English Dictionary*, cited in Ewens, 2014, p 158). These attitudes and aspirations are derived from various sources, including school governors, policy makers, policy regulators and other stakeholders, and this includes you as an employee of the school. As a professional, you have a responsibility and, according to Ofsted (2014), a regulatory requirement to:

○   create a positive climate for learning in which children are interested and engaged;

○   promote an inclusive and positive learning environment.

There are many ways in which you can help your school to meet Ofsted's requirements, including working willingly and enthusiastically with others in a team. Demonstrating positive values, attitudes and behaviour (as outlined in HLTA standard 3 – TDA, 2007, p 96) is important because your actions and your approaches to working with others are likely to be modelled, to some extent, by the children during their own development in relation to working in teams. Teamwork gets the job done as team members support each other and often go the extra mile to achieve success and not let the team down.

Question

What can you do to support your school?

Answer

You can make sure that you know the school procedures and what the school needs to meet its mission and strategy. You can contribute to reviews, special events and parents' evenings. You can also attend in-house or external training events and utilise your strengths to support the school. You need to ensure that you are as up to date as possible with any necessary training and regulatory requirements regarding the support that you can give to children with specific educational needs. If necessary, you should liaise with your line manager about possible training or conferences that you could attend. However, your teacher and the school SENCO should also be able to offer you advice that is specific to the children/child that you are supporting, and they may also be able to give you regular updates on any new regulations that impact on the type of support you are giving. Of course, you can also carry out some research yourself via the internet or the library.

Ofsted inspectors look to see how TAs and other support workers are deployed in general and how they are utilised to support children with SEN. (For more information about safeguarding, see Chapter 4.)

 # Check your understanding

1. If (due to doing other duties) you went into your class a little late, would you know what you had to do, or would you have to wait until the teacher had finished talking with the children so that they could set you a task to do?

2. How has your perception of your role changed since you started your job?

3. How do you envisage your role changing in the light of any current and/or perceived developments relating to:

   ○ the school where you currently work?

   ○ specific regulatory requirements and/or policy?

▶▶ TAKING IT FURTHER

Constable D (2013) *A Teaching Assistant's Pocket Book* (2nd edn). Hampshire: Teachers' Pocketbooks.

Russell, A, Webster, R and Blatchford, P (2013) *Maximising the Impact of Teaching Assistants: Guidance for School Leaders and Teachers*. Oxon: Routledge.

Tomlinson P and Davison, C (2013) *Early Years Policy and Practice*. Northwich: Critical Publishing.

REFERENCES

Belbin, M (1993) *Team Roles at Work*. Oxford: Butterworth-Heinemann.

Coleman, J S (1988) Social Capital in the Creation of Human Capital, Organizations and Institutions. *The American Journal of Sociology: Sociological and Economic Approaches to the Analysis of Social Structure*, 94(Supplement): 95–120.

Cremin, H, Thomas, G and Vincent, K (2003) Learning Zones: An Evaluation of Three Models for Improving Learning Through Teacher/Teaching Assistant Teamwork. *Support for Learning*, 18(4): 154–61.

DfE (2012) *Team Around the Child (TAC)*. [online] Avaliable at: http://webarchive. nationalarchives.gov.uk/20130903161404/http://www.education.gov.uk/ childrenandyoungpeople/strategy/integratedworking/a0068944/team-around-the-child-tac (accessed August, 2014).

Ewens, T (2014) *Reflective Primary Teaching*. Northwich: Critical Publishing.

Groom, B and Rose, R (2005) Supporting the Inclusion of Pupils with Social, Emotional and Behavioral Difficulties in the Primary School: The Role of Teaching Assistants. *Journal of Research in Special Educational Needs*, 5(1): 20–30.

Hay McBer (2000) *Research into Teacher Effectiveness: A Model of Teacher Effectiveness*. (DfEE Research Report 216) London, DfEE.

Janis, I L (1982). *Groupthink: Psychological Studies of Policy Decisions and Fiascoes* (2nd edn). New York: Houghton Mifflin.

Lave, J and Wenger, E (2003) *Situated Learning: Legitimate Peripheral Participation (Learning in doing, social, cognitive and computational perspectives)*. New York: Cambridge University Press.

National Careers Service (2012) *A Service of the Skills Funding Agency on Behalf of the Department for Business, Innovation and Skills*. [online] Available at: https://nationalcareersservice.direct.gov.uk/advice/planning/jobprofiles/Pages/ teachingassistant.aspx (accessed August 2014).

Ofsted (2014) *A Framework for School Inspection*. Manchester: Ofsted, Reference no: 120100. [online] Avaliable at: www.ofsted.gov.uk/resources/130128 (accessed July 2014).

Training and Development Agency for Schools (TDA) (2007) *Higher Level Teaching Assistant Candidate Handbook*. London: TDA. [online] Available at: www.education.gov.uk/ publications/eOrderingDownload/TDA0420.pdf [accessed August 2014].

Woodward, M and Peart, A (2006) *Supporting Education, The Role of Higher Level Teaching Assistants*. London: The Association of Teachers and Lecturers.

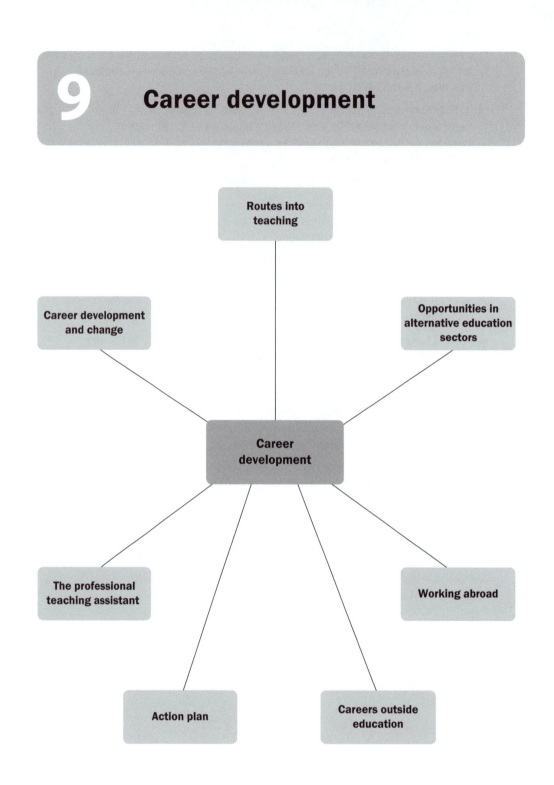

9 **Career development**

Routes into teaching

Career development and change

Opportunities in alternative education sectors

Career development

The professional teaching assistant

Working abroad

Action plan

Careers outside education

HLTA STANDARDS

This chapter links to the following HLTA standards (Training and Development Agency for Schools (TDA), 2007, p 97):

4: communicate effectively and sensitively with children, young people, colleagues, parents and carers;

5: recognise and respect the contribution that parents and carers can make to the development and well-being of children and young people;

6: demonstrate commitment to collaborative and co-operative working with colleagues;

7: improve own knowledge and practice including responding to advice and feedback.

INTRODUCTION

This chapter helps you to evaluate your roles, responsibilities and rights as a teaching assistant (TA). As well as reflecting on how you can develop your practice, you will be able to consider further career opportunities that build on the transferable professional skills you have developed. This chapter focuses on progression routes based on the English education system.

STARTING POINT

○   How would you define professionalism?

○   To what extent does your current role meet your definition of professionalism?

○   Have you considered where you see yourself in one year and in five years' time?

○   What are your ambitions in relation to your own education and career?

THE PROFESSIONAL TEACHING ASSISTANT

In the best schools, well-deployed teaching assistants support teachers in achieving excellent results with pupils.

(DfE, 2010, p 25)

Even if you are not a Higher Level Teaching Assistant (HLTA), HLTA standards offer a useful summary of many if not all of your achievements in your role as well as future developmental aspirations.

Question

What are the five key areas of the HLTA standards (TDA, 2007)?

Answer

The 33 HLTA standards are organised into the following key areas:

o   professional attributes;

o   professional knowledge and understanding;

o   planning and expectations;

o   monitoring and assessment;

o   teaching and learning activities.

The continuing existence of TAs as an integral part of the English education system came under threat following an influential report by the Reform think tank (2010), which argued that TAs were an inefficient use of resources. According to *The Sunday Times* (Woolf and Griffiths, 2013), moves to phase out the role were subsequently considered, though the report's conclusions differed from the original research report, which recommended changes in how TAs were deployed rather than their phased withdrawal (Blatchford et al, 2009). The development and implementation of a new set of standards pencilled in for 2015 suggests that the TA role will remain (DfE, 2014a). This renewed political commitment is articulated by the Minister for Schools, David Laws:

> *Good teaching assistants are essential to driving up standards in the classroom and helping students fulfil their full potential.*

> (DfE, 2014a)

The DfE's (2014a) standards proposal has several aims, notably to:

o   include all TAs within the standards framework;

o   graduate the standards, so that not all of the standards are initially applicable to less qualified/experienced TAs;

o   enable the standards to be used in performance management to help evaluate your contribution to the school;

o   inform your career development needs as a TA.

These standards, once implemented, should therefore play an important role in terms of defining your professional practice as well as guiding your professional development.

Your rights as a professional

Your employment contract explains your rights, roles and responsibilities as a TA, according to organisational requirements and national legislation. This might include guidance on your right to belong to a recognised union such as Unison or the National Association of Schoolmasters Union of Women Teachers (NASUWT). You should request clarification on any issues you have with your contract prior to formal acceptance, regardless of what sort of contract you are on (such as permanent, temporary, fixed or zero hours).

The Equality Act (2010): Protection from bullying, harassment and victimisation

Your employer is also subject to the Equality Act (UK Government, 2010). This protects you from discrimination, harassment or victimisation. Therefore you must not be discriminated against (treated less favourably) due to any of the specific protected characteristics identified in the Act:

○ age;

○ disability;

○ gender reassignment;

○ marriage and civil partnership;

○ pregnancy and maternity;

○ race;

○ religion and belief;

○ sex;

○ sexual orientation.

Discrimination may be direct – explicitly due to the above characteristics – or indirect. Indirect discrimination is the use of an apparently neutral practice, provision or criterion that puts people with a particular protected characteristic at a disadvantage compared with others when applying that practice, provision or criterion cannot be objectively justified. Harassment is defined by EHRC (2014b) as *'Unwanted behaviour that has the purpose or effect of violating a person's dignity or creates a degrading, humiliating, hostile, intimidating or offensive environment.'* Such behaviour focused on the above protected characteristics is unlawful according to the Equality Act (2010).

Victimisation is where a person is treated less favourably due to having made a complaint, or the organisation believing that they are about to make a complaint (otherwise known as *whistleblowing*). If you are aware of a serious issue where your organisation may be in breach of legislation – such as a safeguarding issue – it is your legal responsibility to report this. Many organisations have a written *whistleblowing* policy that you should follow, but if you consider that you have been victimised by an individual such as a manager or the management as a whole as a result of speaking out, the Equality Act (2010) and Public Interest Disclosure Act (1998, cited in ATL, 2014) aim to afford you legal protection.

Redundancy

You may find that your school or academy chain needs to make redundancies, often to reduce costs or relating to curriculum changes. In such a case, it is vital that you are fully aware of the legal procedures that need to be followed, including your rights. As well as protection afforded by the Equality Act (2010, cited in EHRC, 2014a), as summarised above, ATL (2011, p 3) summarises key principles that employers are expected to follow in order to comply with the Employment Rights Act (1996):

○   to warn the workforce of the possibility of redundancies as early as possible;

○   to consult recognised trade unions in good time where 20 or more staff are affected;

○   to establish objective criteria for selection of staff for redundancy;

○   to apply the criteria objectively so that fair selections are made;

○   to take reasonable steps to find alternative employment for displaced staff.

In terms of the redundancy selection process, a decision cannot be made on the basis of discrimination against a protected characteristic as defined in the Equality Act (2010).

Question

A school needs to reduce costs and it chooses to retain its male TA and makes a female TA redundant. She has previously told colleagues that she is planning to have children so the school argues that it would not be able to afford the potential costs of maternity leave. Is this legal? Why/why not?

Answer

This decision is likely to run counter to legislation. Sex (gender) as well as pregnancy and maternity are specifically cited as protected characteristics in the Equality Act and therefore are not legal grounds for redundancy (or recruitment). Furthermore, this decision does not seem to have been based on objective grounds for selection, so could also be against the Employment Rights Act (1996). According to ATL (2011), if you have been made redundant you have up to three months to challenge this decision through an employment tribunal (see Taking it further).

CAREER DEVELOPMENT AND CHANGE

Being a TA is a fantastic role in which you can continue to develop your professional expertise throughout your career. However, the following section considers some of the alternative career opportunities that may interest you. Since 2010, requirements for working within the English education system have changed radically and continue to do so. It's therefore really important that you check the latest guidance on education careers. The Taking it further section provides links to help you keep up to date. As education policy is devolved, you should seek specific guidance from the relevant departments if you are working in Northern Ireland, Wales or Scotland.

Higher Level Teaching Assistant

Higher Level Teaching Assistants (HLTAs) were introduced in 2003 as a means of enabling TAs to take on further responsibilities and reduce the workload of teachers. This might be something you would like to consider. The role might include taking classes without a teacher present, including covering staff absence. Your salary should therefore be higher than as a TA, but terms and conditions vary widely for this role, so it is worth checking these carefully first. To become an HLTA, you need to have a nationally recognised level 2 qualification in English and mathematics and be able to demonstrate that you are meeting all of the HLTA standards. You also need to already be in the TA role and have the support of your school. Your school should help you to identify further training needs to meet the standards, or signpost you to providers who can do this (see Taking it further).

Special Educational Needs Teaching Assistant

A Special Educational Needs Teaching Assistant (SENTA) will have specialist training and experience of supporting children with special educational needs. In this role you will be working directly with a Special Educational Needs Co-ordinator (SENCO).

ROUTES INTO TEACHING

Having worked as a TA you will have observed the role of the teacher and may feel ready to take this on yourself. You shouldn't feel pressurised into doing so – the role of the teacher is different rather than necessarily better. However, if you are interested in becoming a teacher, the following is a brief overview of some of your options. There may be further developments to teaching requirements, so always carefully and regularly check requirements from the Department for Education (see Taking it further).

Primary schools: Qualified Teacher Status

To start any route into gaining primary Qualified Teacher Status (QTS), you currently need to have a university degree as well as at least a GCSE grade C or equivalent in mathematics, English and a science. As part of the application process, you also have to pass professional skills tests in literacy and numeracy (DfE, 2014b). Following the Education Act (UK Government, 2011), there have been numerous changes to the routes into teaching that offer alternatives to the traditional university work-based Post Graduate Certificate in Education (PGCE) programmes. Schools Direct is aimed at graduates, usually with three years' work experience, aiming to change career into teaching. Teach First has been expanded and focuses on recruiting new graduates with high qualifications. Although the qualification is the same, Schools Direct and Teach First focus on in-house training from within a placement school (DfE, 2014c). If you already have a degree and have experience working within a school, you may be able to gain QTS via an assessment-only route (DfE, 2014d). Finally, if you are already a qualified teacher from the European Union, Australia, Canada, New Zealand or the USA you may be able to gain QTS without further requirements (DfE, 2014e).

Along the way to achieving QTS, roles such as HLTA may help you gain the breadth of experience to support your professional development. Regardless of which route is chosen, all applicants have to pass subject skills tests. Following successful qualification, your first year will be as a Newly Qualified Teacher (NQT) (DfE, 2014f), during which time you need to demonstrate your ability to meet the Teachers' Standards (DfE, 2013).

OPPORTUNITIES IN ALTERNATIVE EDUCATION SECTORS

Academies, private schools and free schools

Following the Education Act (2011), academies and free schools have similar authority to private schools in terms of setting their own qualification requirements for teachers. Therefore you may be able to work in these institutions without having completed traditional teacher training qualifications. For example, if you have a specific skill (such as foreign language fluency) a school may consider that this is sufficient for employment, especially on a part-time basis. Gaining further qualifications might become a part of your contract. However, if you are moving from the maintained sector, the established policies and practices may be different from what you are used to, so carefully check your contract for what your duties, responsibilities and rewards are (ATL, 2013a).

Further education and skills (14–19 and adults)

As large organisations, further education (FE) colleges often have many opportunities for career development with differing administrative and education roles frequently coming available. Therefore, gaining any role within such an organisation can be a useful stepping stone for your future development. In FE, the TA role may be known as a Learning Support Assistant (LSA), but other roles may also be suitable. For example, learning mentors may focus on one-to-one work with learners with specific needs. Such roles can lead to opportunities to expand your role into teaching.

Within FE, lecturers can teach without having any teaching qualifications. Between 2007 and 2011 there was a mandatory requirement for new teachers to work towards gaining a teaching qualification while in service. However, following deregulation (UK Government, 2013), there is currently no formal qualification requirement to teach in the FE sector as employment criteria are at the discretion of the provider. Nevertheless, the Certificate in Education and Training (CET) and Diploma in Education and Training (DET) are the nationally recognised teaching qualifications and many providers may expect you to complete these in service as part of your contract (Machin, Hindmarch, Murray and Richardson, 2013, 2014). After gaining the DET qualification, teachers in this sector may work towards gaining Qualified Teacher Learning and Skills (QTLS), which has equivalence to QTS at the discretion of individual providers and authorities (DfE, 2014f). QTLS application was organised though the Institute for Learning (IfL), which closed in 2014, though this may be taken on by the Education and Training Foundation (ETF, see Taking it further).

Assessors and examination markers

Although it can become a career choice in itself, engaging in part-time work as an assessor or examiner can be a useful and flexible means of supplementing your income. Many exams are now marked online, so you don't have to worry about finding office space at home for piles of scripts. You will probably be paid per script marked, and you may have to commit to marking a minimum number of scripts during a set time period. This means that your examining work may be fairly intensive for short periods of time but not in demand throughout the year, meaning that it does not tend to provide a regular or set income.

Each awarding organisation (AO) will have its own recruitment requirements, so investigate these to see if they have any vacancies that suit your skills and knowledge. AOs in the UK include the Assessment and Qualifications Alliance (AQA), City & Guilds and Pearson Edexcel. If you are able to travel around the country (or even abroad), face-to-face examiner posts may be available, with language assessments run by organisations such as Cambridge English and Trinity College London (see Taking it further).

One-to-one tutor

One-to-one tutors are a popular means by which parents help their children to develop their skills, especially in preparation for an exam, for example. Alternatively, adults are often interested in quickly developing skills such as learning a foreign language and are often prepared to pay for one-to-one tuition.

Question

What do you think are the advantages and challenges of one-to-one teaching?

Answer

Working as a one-to-one tutor enables you to gain lesson and curriculum planning and teaching skills in a potentially less stressful environment than the classroom. As with examining, although this is unlikely to be a career in itself, such work can be financially rewarding and a useful supplement to your wages. It may also give you the confidence to set up your own private tutoring business.

You must ensure that terms are clearly agreed in a written contract beforehand and check that such work does not represent a conflict of interest with your school (ATL, 2013b). If parents find you to be a good tutor, word may spread quickly. Try to arrange your tuition into clear blocks so that you don't find yourself teaching virtually every evening. For example, three 1-hour sessions on one evening will be far less strain on you than if they are spread over three evenings. Such blocking also acts as an incentive for punctuality as tutees will miss tuition time if they know someone else is coming straight after. Remember to consider the costs of room hire, transport and so on to ensure that what you are doing is financially worthwhile. If the learner is studying in a private house, this raises potentially serious health and safety, insurance and safeguarding concerns (ATL, 2013b).

Make sure you get your charging right from the start – it's harder to increase your charges once you have started teaching. If the tutee doesn't want to pay they can find someone else – do not work for what you consider to be inadequate compensation. What is important is what your time is worth to you, including how much you will have to pay in tax. For example, £20 an hour might initially sound attractive, but what does this *actually* represent when you consider lesson preparation time and travel time and cost as well as tax deductions? Indeed, ATL (2013b) recommends that you consider a higher figure than this, but whatever you charge, don't settle for less than what you value for your time. Finally, remember that while your tax is probably deducted at source in your school-based work, you are responsible for paying tax on any private work to HM Revenue and Customs (see Taking it further).

Informal and community learning

Remember that education does not take place only in schools and colleges. Your skills might be suitable to train to become involved in youth work, counselling, 'third sector' provision (charities and voluntary organisations), sports coaching and so on. Furthermore, many private companies also run in-house training for staff – for which your experience as an educator might be suitable.

WORKING ABROAD

Working abroad can be a fascinating way of developing your professional skills at the same time as broadening your horizons. There are many opportunities to teach English as a Foreign Language (EFL) throughout the world. You are not usually expected to be fluent in the local language as English is often learned through immersion, that is, using only English in the classroom rather than translation. Alternatively, being an English Language Assistant enables you to support a local teacher in the classroom.

With either role, experience teaching or assisting abroad looks great on your curriculum vitae (CV) as it demonstrates your flexibility as well as vital transferable skills (British Council, 2014):

○   cultural awareness;

○   communication and presentation;

○   creative thinking and problem solving;

○   time management and organisation;

○   working alone and as part of a team.

In addition, there is the potential to gain valuable foreign language skills.

Each country will have different expectations in terms of qualifications and experience. It is possible to earn a good wage while working abroad, but pay and conditions widely vary between countries. In many countries work might entail a 'living wage' – often sufficient for a reasonable standard of living in that country but not sufficient for saving due to a poor currency exchange rate. A great source of information about teaching EFL abroad can be found at the British Council. It is also a good idea to gain a short EFL qualification that will ground you in the basics. There are many weekend or online Teaching English as a Foreign Language courses available. These may serve as a useful introduction to the subject, but are probably not adequate to meet the qualification needs of the country's education system that you intend to work in. An internationally recognised qualification is the Cambridge Certificate in English Language Teaching to Adults, with an optional extension module for teaching young learners. You should therefore carefully check with the British Council about the value and international recognition of any qualification you are considering (see Taking it further).

CAREERS OUTSIDE EDUCATION

Return to the notes that you made about your roles and responsibilities at the beginning of the chapter.

Question

What skills and qualities do you possess to fulfil your professional role?

Answer

Your answer might include:

- the ability to communicate with fellow professionals and children;
- teamworking;
- administration;
- creativity;
- enthusiasm;
- adaptability and flexibility;
- numeracy and literacy skills.

Question

What alternative careers might these suit?

Answer

As an education professional you are developing employability skills that will enable you to enter a wide range of fields. Just because your experience of work is in a school, this shouldn't stop you considering other jobs in the private or public sectors. Focus on the skills you have, rather than where you gained them, in order to open up new possibilities for your career.

ACTION PLAN

To help you focus on your future development aspirations, you may find that an action plan is a useful means of organising necessary tasks into manageable 'SMART' steps. SMART is a commonly used acronym to help clarify objectives and means: specific, measurable, achievable, relevant and time-bound.

Activity

Construct an action plan based on your key professional development targets. An example is provided in Table 9.1.

Table 9.1 Example professional development plan

Aim	Objectives (individual steps to achieve this aim)	Potential barriers and how these can be overcome	Deadline	Progress to date
eg gain HLTA	Investigate HLTA guidance	Don't know where to start Ask colleagues who are HLTAs for guidance	May	Been given standards and looked at opportunities for assessment
	Discuss opportunities to develop role with manager	Discuss at my next appraisal meeting	July	Meeting time and date arranged. Requested to discuss HLTA
	Achieve level 2 mathematics	Lack confidence with mathematics Discuss how colleagues achieved this. Join level 2 night class	Sept–May	Found possible courses

 Check your understanding

1. The Equality Act (2010, cited in EHRC, 2014a) protects you from discrimination, harassment or victimisation in the workplace. It is important to understand the legal definitions of these terms, so visit the EHRC website for a thorough explanation (see Taking it further).

2. Check career and training development options in your school/area.

▶▶ **TAKING IT FURTHER**

UK education departments

England (schools): Department for Education: www.gov.uk/government/
organisations/department-for-education.

(Further and Higher Education): Department for Business Innovation and Skills (BIS):
www.gov.uk/government/organisations/department-for-business-innovation-
skills (accessed October 2014).

Northern Ireland: Department of Education Northern Ireland: www.deni.gov.uk/
(accessed October 2014).

Scotland: The Learning Directorate: www.scotland.gov.uk/About/People/
Directorates/learning (accessed October 2014).

Wales: Department for Education and Skills: wales.gov.uk/topics/
educationandskills/?lang=en (accessed October 2014).

Exam boards

AQA: www.aqa.org.uk (accessed September 2014).

Cambridge Assessment (2014) Careers: www.cambridgeassessment.org.uk/careers/
(accessed September 2014).

HLTA information

Best Practice Net *Preparation for Assessment for HLTA Status*. www.bestpracticenet.
co.uk/hlta (accessed August 2014).

Guidance on your rights and unions for TAs

ATL: *New to Teaching*: www.new2teaching.org.uk/ (accessed August 2014).

ATL: *Factsheets*: www.atl.org.uk/publications-and-resources/factsheets/all-atl-
factsheets.asp (accessed July 2014).

ATL: *Legal and Employment*: www.new2teaching.org.uk/tzone/your-union/
publications/legal-employment.asp (accessed August 2014).

EHRC: *Guidance for Workers*: www.equalityhumanrights.com/your-rights/
employment/guidance-workers (accessed September 2014).

NASUWT: *Teaching Assistant*: www.nasuwt.org.uk/MemberSupport/TeacherGroups/
TeachingAssistant/ (accessed September 2014).

Unison: *A Quick Guide to Unison*: www.unison.org.uk/about/ (accessed September
2014).

Teacher training

Early Years

Musgrave, J and Stobbs, N (2015) *Early Years Placements*. Northwich: Critical
Publishing.

Schools

DfE Teacher Training: What Are My Options? www.education.gov.uk/get-into-teaching/teacher-training-options.aspx?sc_lang=en-GB (accessed August 2014).

Northern Ireland: Teacher qualifications and registration: www.deni.gov.uk/index/school-staff/teachers-teachinginnorthernireland_pg.htm (accessed October 2014).

Owen, D and Burnett, C (2014) *Getting into Primary Teaching*. Northwich: Critical Publishing.

Scotland: Teachers: www.teachinscotland.org/ (accessed January 2015).

University of Buckingham: The Good Teacher Training Guide: www.buckingham.ac.uk/research/ceer (accessed September 2014).

Wales: Teacher Training and Education in Wales/Hyfforddiant Athrawon ac Addysg yng Nghymru: http://teachertrainingcymru.org/index.htm (accessed October 2014).

Further education

ETF Support for Teacher Recruitment: www.et-foundation.co.uk/supporting/support-teacher-recruitment/ (accessed September 2014).

Education in the News

The Guardian: www.theguardian.com/education (accessed September 2014).

TES: www.tes.co.uk/ (accessed September 2014).

Working abroad

British Council (2014) *Teach English*: www.britishcouncil.org/teach-english (accessed August 2014).

British Council (2014) *Why Become a Language Assistant?* www.britishcouncil.org/language-assistants/become (accessed August 2014).

Thornbury, S and Watkins, P (2007) *The Certificate in English Language Teaching to Adults Course*. Cambridge: Cambridge University Press.

REFERENCES

Anon. (2014) Becoming a Higher Level Teaching Assistant. *Times Educational Supplement*. [online] Available at: www.tes.co.uk/article.aspx?storyCode=6166885 (accessed August 2014).

ATL (2011) Redundancy. [online] Available at: www.atl.org.uk/publications-and-resources/legal-employment-advice/redundancy.asp (accessed August 2014).

ATL (2013a) ATL Advice: Private Tuition. [online] Available at: www.atl.org.uk/publications-and-resources/factsheets/private-tuition.asp (accessed January 2015).

ATL (2013b) Working in an Academy. [online] Available at: www.atl.org.uk/working-in-an-academy.asp (accessed January 2015).

ATL (2014) ATL Advice: Whistleblowing. [online] Available at: www.atl.org.uk/publicationsand-resources/factsheets/whistleblowing.asp (accessed May 2014).

Blatchford, P, Bassett, P, Brown, P, Martin, C, Russell, A and Webster, R (2009) *Deployment and Impact of Support Staff*. London: DfCSF. [online] Available at: www.teachingassistantresearch.co.uk/the-diss-project/4581705268 (accessed October 2014).

British Council (2014) *Why Become a Language Assistant?* [online] Available at: www.britishcouncil.org/language-assistants/become/why-become-language-assistant (accessed August 2014).

DfE (2010) *The Importance of Teaching*. London: DfE. [online] Available at: www.gov.uk/government/uploads/system/uploads/attachment_data/file/175429/CM-7980.pdf (accessed September 2014).

DfE (2013) *Teachers' Standards*. London: DfE. [online] Available at: www.gov.uk/government/publications/teacher-standards (accessed January 2015).

DfE (2014a) *Review of Standards for Teaching Assistants Launched*. London: DfE. [online] Available at: www.gov.uk/government/news/review-of-standards-for-teaching-assistants-launched (accessed October 2014).

DfE (2014b) Professional Skills Tests for Trainee Teachers. [online] Available at: www.education.gov.uk/get-into-teaching/apply-for-teacher-training/skills-tests (accessed January 2015).

DfE (2014c) School-Led Teacher Training. [online] Available at: www.education.gov.uk/get-into-teaching/teacher-training-options/school-based-training (accessed January 2015).

DfE (2014d) *Assessment Only (AO) Route to QTS*. www.education.gov.uk/get-into-teaching/teacher-training-options/assessment-only (accessed October 2014).

DfE (2014e) Information for Teachers Qualified in Australia, Canada, New Zealand and the USA. [online] Available at: www.education.gov.uk/get-into-teaching/teacher-training-options/australia-canada-nz-usa (accessed October 2014).

DfE (2014f) What Happens After I Qualify? [online] Available at: www.education.gov.uk/get-into-teaching/about-teaching/induction-year (accessed January 2015).

EHRC (2014a) Protected Characteristics. [online] Available at: www.equalityhumanrights.com/private-and-public-sector-guidance/guidance-all/protected-characteristics (accessed September 2014).

EHRC (2014b) Glossary of Terms. [online] Available at: www.equalityhumanrights.com/private-and-public-sector-guidance/guidance-all/glossary-terms (accessed January 2015).

HLTA National Assessment Partnership HLTA Standards. [online] Available at: http://hlta.org.uk/node/104 (accessed September 2014).

Machin, L, Hindmarch, D, Murray, S and Richardson, T (2013) *A Complete Guide to the Level 4 Certificate in Education and Training*. Northwich: Critical Publishing.

Machin, L, Hindmarch, D, Murray, S and Richardson, T (2014) *A Complete Guide to the Level 5 Diploma in Education and Training*. Northwich: Critical Publishing.

Training and Development Agency for Schools (TDA) (2007) *Higher Level Teaching Assistant candidate handbook*. London: Training and Development Agency for Schools. [online] Available at: www.education.gov.uk/publications/eOrderingDownload/TDA0420.pdf (accessed January 2015).

UK Government (2010) *The Equality Act*. London: HM Government. [online] Available at: www.legislation.gov.uk/ukpga/2010/15/pdfs/contents (accessed January 2015).

UK Government (2011) *The Education Act*. London: HM Government. [online] Available at: www.legislation.gov.uk/ukpga/2011/21/contents/enacted (accessed September 2011).

UK Government (2013) *The Further Education Teachers' Qualifications (England) (Revocation) Regulations (2013)*. [online] Available at: www.legislation.gov.uk/uksi/2013/1976/contents/made (accessed September 2013).

Woolf, M and Griffiths, S (2013) 230,000 Classroom Assistants Face the Axe. *The Sunday Times*, 2 June. [online] Available at: www.thesundaytimes.co.uk/sto/news/uk_news/Education/article1268217.ece (accessed January 2015).

Index